Akashic Records Revelation

Unlock the healing power of your untethered soul and raise your vibration; read and access the quantum field to unleash your cosmic consciousness

By Sharon Copeland

© **Copyright 2021 - All rights reserved.**

The content contained within this book may not be reproduced, duplicated, or transmitted without direct written permission from the author or the publisher.

Under no circumstances will any blame or legal responsibility be held against the publisher, or author, for any damages, reparation, or monetary loss due to the information contained within this book; either directly or indirectly.

Legal Notice

This book is Copyright protected. It is only for personal use. You cannot amend, distribute, sell, use, quote, or paraphrase any part of the content within this book, without the consent of the author or publisher.

Disclaimer Notice

Please note the information contained within this document is for educational and entertainment purposes only. All effort has been executed to present accurate, up-to-date, reliable, complete information. No warranties of any kind are declared or implied. Readers acknowledge that the author is not engaged in the rendering of legal, financial, medical, or professional advice. The content within this book has been derived from various sources.

Please consult a licensed professional before attempting any techniques outlined in this book.

Table of Contents

Akashic Records Revelation 1

Introduction 7

Free Audiobook 9

Free Workbook 10

Chapter 1 11

What Are The Akashic Records? 11

    How can we gain access to the Akashic Records? 14

    What could be gained from the Akashic Records? 15

Chapter 2 16

Guidelines For Reading the Akashic Records 16

    Just how can you enter the Akashic Records? 17

    What takes place when you open the Akashic Records? 18

    Benefits of working with the Akashic Records 18

    Will you have a bad experience when entering the Akashic Records? 19

    Is there any preparation you need to do before you have a reading with a professional Akashic Record reader? 20

    Is there more preparation you need to do before you can check the Records for yourself? 20

    Are you prepared to work with the Akashic Records? 20

Chapter 3 23

The Akashic Records on the Quantum Field 23

    Information 26

Chapter 4 29

Akashic Records and Claiming your Power 29

    Akashic Records Wisdom 29

The power of the Akashic Records 31

The strength of your story in the Akashic Records 33

Chapter 5 36

Accessing Others' Akashic Records 36

How can you figure out how to flip through the Akashic Records? 40

What's a method of accessing the records? 41

Can anyone enter the Akashic Records? 41

So, how can you get information from the Akashic Records? 42

Accessing the Akashic Records 42

Astounding insights you can gain if you read a person's akashic record. 44

Chapter 6 52

Healing Within the Akashic Records 52

How can accessing Akashic Records heal? 53

What can they heal? 54

Will you experience healing by using the Akashic Records? 54

Chapter 7 57

Using the Akashic Records to Heal Yourself 57

Ten ways the Akashic Records can heal your life 58

Healing at a soul level 61

Chapter 8 64

Healing Past Lives in the Akashic Records 64

How would you define a past life? 65

Exactly how can our past life help us heal the soul? 65

Can it be feasible for past life or perhaps a parallel life to affect our current life? How? 66

Past lives now guide us to the Akashic Records 66

Who can access the Akashic Records? 67

Just how can I access the Akashic Records?..67

Remembering past-lives 69

Chapter 9..72

Meditation and the Akashic Records..72

How about meditation posture?...77

The real difference between meditation as well as the Akashic Records........80

Chapter 10..83

Reading the Akashic Records 83

What are Akashic Record readings? What can I expect from them?..............85

Preparing for an Akashic Records reading..85

Sample questions to ask the Akashic Records..86

Benefits of accessing your Akashic Records...88

Obvious obstacles to your present life 89

Expand your awareness: Reconnect to the source.......................................89

Chapter 11..91

Akashic Records of the Future 91

Open your soul's path 92

The way the future is changing in your Akashic Records 92

Akashic consultation vs. Psychic reading 94

Are there questions the Akashic Records can't answer?...............................98

Conclusion 103

Introduction

The Akashic Field is a field of infinite possibilities; a field beyond time and space from which everything emerges and is an experiential body of compassion and knowledge. We're talking about potentials here, which is exactly why when we tap into this particular source of knowledge, we're in a position to grasp an insight into the possibilities on our path. From there, we can alter timelines and shift paths for the ultimate empowerment and development of our souls. I consider it as researching our soul's potential; an investigation.

Akashic Records exist to all who seek them. It's your divine right. Compassionate energy and the love that the Akasha has prepared for you. Often, individuals experience doubt, afraid that they will not do something "right", or fearing what energy they could open themselves up to, the list goes on. This program will push you through that, supporting your connection and helping you build your foundation so that you are ready to go into action and feel confident in your relationship with this spiritual tool.

The Akashic Field, also referred to on its own as Akashic, is a field of life force that permeates and structures the universe in its entirety; from the smallest particle to the biggest star and most of the laws which govern it. Since the start of all things, it's existed. Experts from a wide range of areas, who currently work on aspects of the Theory of TOE (or Theory of Everything) are beginning to recognize that this particular field exists and is as necessary, and ever-present, as electromagnetics or gravity. Their theories, studies, and conclusions lead many of them to understand its existence, something that indigenous cultures all over the earth have known for millennia. This life isn't all present in the universe and being physical is just part of what we are.

The Akashic Records is where information about every little thing that is currently present or has possibly ever existed, is kept. As we contain the memories of what we've experienced and where we've come from, the Akashic will also keep a memory of everything. Each soul, each being, has a record of all they have been and all they currently are. Most medicine experts, psychics, and spiritual beings reach out when helping people seek guidance or perhaps benefit from many other realms. Each soul's record, what I term a Soul Book, contains an entire historical record of the experiences they've had, their plans for their current incarnation, and the continuing history of life in this physical form.

Free Audiobook

Akashic Records Revelation Audiobook is now available too! Get your free copy now on Audible at the following link!

https://swiy.io/ARAudio

Or scan this code with your phone's camera

Free Workbook

To help you take some "me" time and reflect on what actions to take after reading this book, I have prepared a workbook with some key questions to ask yourself. I hope this helps!

You can find the workbook by following the link below:

https://swiy.io/AkashicRecordsWorkbookLP

Or scan this code with your phone's camera

Chapter 1

What Are The Akashic Records?

"If you want to find the secrets of the universe, think in terms of energy, frequency, and vibration"
Nikola Tesla

You might have heard about the Akashic Records, and since been wondering what they are all about. Akashic Records are a library that holds memories of our past, present, and future lives. In this chapter, you'll learn about the history, purpose, and deeper meaning of these records.

When you are not well versed in metaphysics, you may not understand what the Akashic Records are. But you should, because according to those that believe in the presence of these so-called records, every soul has one.

First things first, the word "Akasha" translates in Sanskrit to "atmosphere," which is exactly where said records exist. But why don't we pull back a bit and break down this loaded concept that is not yet backed by scientific evidence? Virtually all of our understanding of it exists in invisible planes and vague ideas. In 1875, a philosopher founded the Theosophy Society. This institution was a place where Helena Blavatsky and her pupils could practice Theosophy; an esoteric "religion" that she led with Henry Steel Olcott, one of the first Americans to fully convert to Buddhism. I have indicated religion in quotes as it is a philosophy of faith, which in itself, is regarded as a way of not just thinking about things, but something to believe in. Together, Olcott and Blavatsky tried to bring their different religious philosophies forward to give spiritualists a bedrock to lean on, philosophies that were outside of Biblical beliefs but related.

Among the philosophies that were able to live on long after Blavatsky, was the concept that there's an invisible life force, or perhaps cosmic light, that records everything we've done, thought, and said. This idea, later on, was described as the "Akashic Records," a spiritual library that is present on just one dimension, yet records all dimensions. For those who are interested in philosophies that require you to believe in the unseeable, you may be ready to embrace and explore this idea as well as access this library. However, if you require facts that are hard and rational explanations, this idea will sound like something that J.K. Rowling created.

The Akashic Records perceive that all matter impressions (everything that actually happened or perhaps existed) are captured in subtle planes. It's the indirect record of the explicit. Others call it the 'memory of nature.' I see it as a figure of speech for organic coding, like DNA.

Why should we care about them, you ask? Because it is a pretty comforting idea when you consider it.

It's the underbelly of reality - a method to explain existence. It is the perception that anything that ever was has a long-lasting imprint on the fabric of reality. The imprints, the effects are made apparent through patterns, like a leaf falling into still water and causing ripples. Both the water and the leaf are forever changed. The leaf's function falling into water has become a part of history; both tangible and cosmic. If you consider yourself the planet and the leaf as the still water, you can expand this theory and see how it establishes our existence by showing that it truly counts.

However, you can wrap your head around the idea, you are probably wondering where you can look for it - and that is a little more complicated. The "where" is a mysterious place. We access it by observing natural patterns. Patterns expose the implicit intelligence of all nature. I love knowing after autumn comes winter. It's recorded, patterns repeat. Clairvoyants and foretellers are masters of prescience; by identifying subtle patterns in our sensate reality, one's instinct becomes a honed skill.

If you would like to know about your very own soul history, you can just turn inward through deep breathing and practice. It is suggested to note patterns in your life, observe patterns in nature, and use your findings to make sense of your existence. All of which states that things are made from something, and one thing can't ever go back to nothing. So, follow your intuition and trace your steps - even if you cannot see them.

The Akashic Records are described in every spiritual tome composed throughout history, often as the Book of Life. These files have been referred to as the Cosmic Mind, the Universal Mind, or the Eye of God. The Akashic Records consist of energy that makes up everything in deep space, so this energy is regarded as the power of love. This energy is described as "Akasha," which originated from the words "Aka," which implies storage place, and "Sa," which means surprise or secret. Probably the most straightforward translation of Akasha is "an unseen space or storage area location."

The Akashic Records are the evidence of your soul's journey, from the valuable time you first arise from the source until you eventually return to the house. The Akashic energy possesses all your thoughts, feelings, deeds, and actions from each lifetime. The Akashic Field is an element of and is hooked up to all, in everything and everyone. You have your very own masters, beings, and teachers of light that keep track of the information unique to you. We can access these teachers and masters, and they will answer your personal questions relating to this life and your past lives that are affecting you today. Our concern is complete Karma, meeting our previous life vows, staying with somebody unique, and supporting individuals who belong to our soul family. Sometimes in our life, we feel blocked or maybe constricted or possibly dissatisfied in our life. We don't remember exactly why we picked our circumstances or households, but the Akashic Records can help you discover these details and allow you to recover and clear your psychological discomfort. You can ask questions about health, life purpose, relationships, career, abundance, and self-esteem.

How can we gain access to the Akashic Records?

The Akashic Records are hidden but may be seen at any time by anyone. Usually, we unknowingly access this data regularly. Whenever you have a flicker of intuition or even a "hunch," you're getting a look into the divine wisdom contained within the Akashic Records.

The Records can be seen through intuition, meditation, and prayer. The most effective way to gain self-access is to intentionally open up to our intuition and inner guidance. This is the supreme way to access what the Akashic Records are attempting to provide the universe; the loving and positive energy of the Records themselves.

For those who aren't experienced with prayer and meditation, or those who just wish to have guidance during this time, an experienced teacher accessing the Akashic Records can be of tremendous help.

What could be gained from the Akashic Records?

If you seek simple information, like "what was I like in my past life?", then you'll be greeted with a lot of information from the Akashic Records. There are many past lives to choose from, so it's crucial to keep in mind that the information we receive won't be the guidance we had expected. Suppose you're ready to accept your problems for what they are and are completely in tune with what you'd love to understand. In that case, you definitely might receive information about relationships, your health, your soul path, and each conceivable alternate topic relating to your daily life. During your Akashic Record reading, you'll also experience the entire spectrum of the Records' energy of love, which will provide you with a hopeful feeling and profound empowerment by knowing the truth of your circumstances and the possibilities unfolding in your life.

Who knew such records existed, right? As mentioned earlier, it is quite comforting to know that there are these memories that we can access anytime. But did you know that you can access these records by yourself? Learn the guidelines for reading the Akashic Records in the next chapter!

Chapter 2

Guidelines For Reading the Akashic Records

"Healing takes courage, and we all have courage, even if we have to dig a little to find it."
Tori Amos

It's often misunderstood that only professionals can read your Akashic Records. The truth is, you can access them on your own in the comfort of your home! In this chapter, get to know the guidelines you need to follow when accessing the library of life!

Though it's thought that the Akashic Records contain all information about events in the past, present, and future, they are valuable for healing and divination. It's also believed some boundaries apply.

Think of searching the Akashic Records in a comparable method to conducting a Google search. You can call up a search for detailed information about recovery and disease, about previous lives, relationships, soul agreements, etc.

Nevertheless, you'll also have to proceed through the filters out of your guides. If your guides don't see you as being prepared to getting a complete view of particular details, you might be blocked from receiving certain information at a given time. This is much like a search being blocked by your computer's antivirus protection.

If you're granted a chance to access the information you're seeking, you may receive information about your connection with others. Your relationship to a friend, lover, and sometimes even an adversary can be described from a greater level.

You might see the core cause of an illness or perhaps an injury about your path along with your higher growth as an individual. You might attempt to search for methods to heal a relationship once you see the job you were destined to play in each other's lives.

Just how can you enter the Akashic Records?

Others believe a guide should enable you to enter the Akashic Records and that you simply want the approval to investigate specific information about your path or even others' paths.

This way, you're kept from delving into information that you're not prepared for, or information that might be counterproductive for you to have.

Other modern gurus will try to inform you there's just one real way or one true prayer that leads to accessing the Akashic Records. This is not true.

Ultimately, we're all psychic beings and the Akashic Records, together with the collective unconscious, links all of us as people with the divine. Thus, no one has permission to access the collective unconscious.

Explore and try to experiment with the various methods and meditations to enable you to reach the Records. You will see for yourself, it's feasible to get into the Records without a guru's assistance.

What takes place when you open the Akashic Records?

It's thought that when one enters the Akashic Records, you can access all information about your previous, present, and future lives, as well as all information about the paths of others. Generally, this particular record is a place where all truths are known.

Experiences may differ from individual to individual, but most often, there's a benevolent guide, being, or perhaps angel, who'll enable you to access the Akashic Records. In addition to this, the spirit will use inviting "language" to convey information.

If you're a film buff, the Records may show up as images on a film screen. If perhaps you're a passionate reader, you might see the Akashic Records as books in a library.

Some describe the feeling as channeling the information from the data through a close relationship with their guides. The more you go to the Akashic Records, the more comfortable and confident you will be in using this channel to unlock higher wisdom.

Benefits of working with the Akashic Records

Working with the Akashic Records can enable you to delve into future potential and past lives. This could improve your psychic ability and enable you to work with other tools like Tarot.

When you work together with the Akashic Records, you are looking at the best view of events. Therefore, the information might be sent in less physical and more symbolic ways.

This may cause a greater understanding and recovery. You might have an emotionally cleansing experience whenever you have a look at the Akashic Records. You may come away with a higher understanding of the issues that resulted in separation.

Will you have a bad experience when entering the Akashic Records?

Like most meditative experiences, the experience of entering the Akashic Records is uplifting and healing.

Suppose you have a "negative" experience in which you feel afraid, nervous, or perhaps motivated to do one thing you would not usually do. In that case, this might be a manifestation of anxiety in your subconscious.

These bad experiences aren't part of accessing the Akashic Records and may suggest discomfort with meditating or unhealing psychological issues that can trigger fearful responses.

If this occurs to you, it could be better to focus on relaxation techniques and meditation before using more specific techniques, like accessing the Akashic Records.

In short, nothing bad can happen. It is like a stream of consciousness, where like sleep talking, one does not think at all. The mind is completely shut off, so it is just coming straight through you, naturally. It does not feel like you have just opened your mouth to speak. It is simply the process of turning your ego off and trusting that whatever is coming through is what needs to come through.

Is there any preparation you need to do before you have a reading with a professional Akashic Record reader?

There is no preparation to do, and I encourage people not to over plan. When you first learn about the records and come into a session or a meeting with me, I will go into your soul. Over planning is missing the point entirely. I always tell people to instinctively flow through appointments and ask themselves, "What is intuitively coming to you since you are tapping into your soul?" or "What exactly do you feel you have to know?". Sometimes people have many questions on their minds, and then the moment the appointment starts, they feel as though they do not wish to ask any of them. Instead, they feel the need to ask something else that has just randomly come through to them."

Is there more preparation you need to do before you can check the Records for yourself?

In order to reach the stage where I could read through the Akashic Records, I peeled back my layers and got to know myself again. After having a baby, I'd begin at the bottom once again and I finally figured out who the heck I was; this was what I had to do to get myself to the stage of reading through the records.

The courses I have developed allow men and women to do the necessary work so that if they wish to read through the records, the access is there for them. The purpose is to align with yourself and trust what is coming through. You do not have to get into the records, and you do not need someone to tell you what you should do. These courses empower you to claim your power back. Naturally, this is a constant journey.

Are you prepared to work with the Akashic Records?

Based on the information above, are you prepared to use your Akashic Records?

In that case, keep in mind that if you work together with the Akashic Records, you're entering into a loving and spiritual realm in which you connect both with your guides as well as your potential. This should feel positive and loving.

Even if you're exploring a hard issue, perhaps a loss or illness, the Akashic Records is a place of love, connection, transformation, and healing.

The more you use this technique to access your higher wisdom, the more improvement you may find in your predictive work, tarot readings, and psychic development.

This is because you're aligning your energy with higher vibrations, and you maintain this higher vibration even outside of the meditation practice. Make sure to sample several various methods of accessing the Akashic Records to notice which one feels most beneficial for you.

You might want to write down or record your experiences during or immediately after the meditation. By doing this, you can jot down or record information that will come to you while it's fresh in your brain.

Because you're altering your consciousness in the meditation process, you might feel as though information came through a dream. You might think you will remember it all, to later find that this is not the case after a couple of minutes pass by.

Therefore, it is great to stop and record your experiences either during (through recording) or perhaps shortly after the meditation.

If a person asks you specifically to seek information on their behalf, continue to allow your guides to be the gatekeepers who allow you to use this information or not.

Never take it upon yourself to attempt to roam into the Records of another individual. Just as you would not sleuth through another person's phone, you don't make use of the Records to explore another's course.

The objective should be about the healing and growth of the individual, not to infringe on the privacy of others.

As you can see, there's not much preparation that you need to do when accessing your records. You just have to be open and accepting of the information that comes to you in the process of prayer or meditation. Now, what is the science behind the Akashic Records? Keep reading to find out its relation to the Quantum Field!

Chapter 3

The Akashic Records on the Quantum Field

"The Akashic Records are the impressions from all of our past lives that are available within our casual body".
Frederick Lenz

Let's talk science! In this chapter, you'll learn more about the Akashic Field and how it gives us the capability to develop our consciousness.

Based on Ervin Laszlo, the galaxies' coherence and the atom are similar to the rationality that keeps living cells together, cooperating to create life. When a complicated system that is comprised of many interacting parts is operating, a surprise jump to a higher level of the complex organization happens. The human body is comprised of such levels, each created by another jump in complexity. Our lowest cell level jumps up a level to body tissue, then to a body organ, then to the body system, and then finally, the entire body. Therefore, just like onions, we're formed with many skins which act as levels that all cooperate in complex ways to create one whole human being. It's truly amazing just how it all fits together.

While doing so, in the human realm of consciousness, we're - as much as we know - the only creatures able to consider who we are, as well as understand the reason of how and where we fit into the universe. This coherence also allows evolution which has enabled us to evolve from a microscopic bacterium to complex beings with all our spiritual, emotional, physical, and mental capabilities.

Ervin Laszlo presents a theory that assists in connecting both. He suggests that the quantum vacuum - which we know contains the entirety of our history from the Big Bang to today - is awareness. For that reason, everything in the universe has consciousness; from a pebble to a tree, to a cloud, to an individual. While this breaks the view of mainstream science, you will discover some highly appreciated researchers like Fritjof Capra, David Bohm, and Freeman Dyson, who support the idea that deep space is, in fact, conscious.

What's consciousness? Consciousness is about being informed of our very own existence and also the environment in which we live. So, if one subatomic particle reacts in line with another particle elsewhere in the universe, we can say it's conscious of what another is doing. In a way, it's conscious of itself in the universe. Thus, the question is: Is it sufficient to point out that all particles in the universe are conscious?

We're aware of our existence and have evolved a brain to access and use the consciousness held in a quantum vacuum. Consciousness is one other manifestation of coherence, allowing a mass of nerve cells to cooperate and create a single sense of self.

Ervin Laszlo compares this quantum vacuum with the Akashic Field of ancient Hindu spiritual tradition. Hindus say the Akashic Record is a field from which most of the universe is formed, and that it holds all that was, is, or perhaps will be. Hindus also point out that the Big Bang that started the universe, and the big crunch that will happen as soon as the universe goes into reverse and collapses back into itself, is just a component of many cycles of universes. It is the same as ours; disappearing and appearing, the same as the subatomic particles in our society.

Ervin Laszlo states that information may be transferred from one cycle to a higher cycle, which describes exactly how the accurate numbers for gravity, electromagnetism, etc, come to be very precise when there hasn't been a time that is enough for these to have formed randomly. Those numbers are transferred from previous universes.

The Akashic Field, being the background on the subatomic worlds, also moves through other realms of stars, human life, and galaxies, and is an activating force in all those realms. It's the force moving the galaxies, the stars, and the spark that gives life to sets of molecules, driving the strength of evolution and giving us the capability to develop our consciousness and experience the unity of the universe.

Ervin Laszlo's theory says we're therefore linked to other individuals who have ever lived, and we can access them by accessing the Akashic Field. This could describe life after death because the past has never disappeared, telling us that the past is ever-present in all things we do. It points to a universe where all is one, as well as how everything is linked. Should we tune ourselves into the Akashic Field, we can access abilities that seem to be supernatural, but are in fact entirely natural. Activities, including meditation, can help us plug into the Akashic Field to allow us to become much more than we are at present. Science and spirituality don't have to be set against one another as we've believed for so long.

Ervin Laszlo associates the world of science with spiritual traditions, presenting it in a logical and seemingly clear way, incorporating the most recent research in many fields of medical research, and tying it completely into a great cohesive theory that makes good sense of numerous, unusual, and contradictory parts of the universe. It describes what's generally called the supernatural in natural terms, providing evidence that supports the reality of such things as clairvoyance, spiritual healing, and reincarnation.

Information

Ervin Laszlo states that within the universe, information is entirely fundamental. In the most recent concept, the universe does not consist of space and matter. Instead, it consists of information and energy. Power is present in the form of wave propagations and wave patterns in the quantum vacuum that fills space; in its many forms, power is the "hardware" of the universe. The application is information. The universe isn't an assemblage of bits of inert matter moving passively in space that is empty; it's a coherent and dynamic whole. The energy that constitutes its hardware is everywhere and always informed. It's formed by what David Bohm called the implicate order and what physicists now regard as the quantum vacuum or zero-point field (also called physical spacetime, universal field). This is the formation that structures the physical world and the information we grasp as nature's laws. Without information, the universe's energy waves and patterns would be unstructured and random, just as a computer's actions would suffer without its software. But the universe is not unstructured and random; it's exactly informed. Would it be any less precisely informed? Complex systems couldn't have emerged in it, and we wouldn't be here to ask just how this extremely unlikely advancement might have happened.

The answer science needs to the 'what' question refers to an entangled, holographic, non-local linking in the universes' development field. In his books - in the biggest detail in Science and the Akashic Field - he discusses this specific field's evidence. He notes that Hindu seers referred to it as Akasha, the essential component of the cosmos. In recognition of this insight, he calls the universe's information field, the Akashic Field.

But how does the logical answer to the question regarding the important significance of the religious experience relate to the answer given by religion?

For the world's religious beliefs, the deeper and larger reality to which the spiritual experience connects us is a numinous, magnificent truth. It's both a spirit and consciousness that instills the natural world (the immanentism view) or possibly a spirit or consciousness that's above and beyond it (the transcendentalist claim). Traditional polytheistic religions favored the former, while the Abrahamic monotheistic faiths (with some exceptions) accepted the latter.

The distinction between an immanent divine intelligence in the planet and one that transcends it's not negligible, but it's still only a difference in interpretation. Both positions' raw data is the same: it's the religious experience, a quantum communion with universal oneness. In the Western religious perspective, this is communion with the spirit that infuses the cosmos, identified as God. Deepak Chopra writes, "*Spirituality is the experience of that domain of consciousness, just where we experience our universality. This domain of consciousness is a core consciousness that is beyond our mind, ego, and intellect. In religious traditions, this core consciousness is described as the soul. That is an element of a collective soul or perhaps collective consciousness, which often is a part of a common domain of consciousness referred to in religions as God.*"

Our belief is that the world's core consciousness is ultimately an experience of the general domain of consciousness. Something that western religions refer to as, God. The belief itself, or even its interpretation, is the same in most religions and in all religions, and it inspires a feeling of wholeness and belonging. When you remove the culture, history, and dogma of every religion, the teachers of those religions teach similar practices and principles that result in a feeling of oneness that ends a sense of separation from the whole.

Science's answer to the issue of what the religious experience connects us to is immanentism. The information which underlies the universe, the Akashic Field, is an element of the universe. This does not indicate that the immanentism position necessarily states the supreme truth; it just means that science can take no more than an immanentism position. Researchers are limited to speaking about the natural world; they must leave speculation about transcendent realities to poets, spiritual masters, and philosophers.

It is time to conclude. If the religious experience's substance is everywhere and always the same, differences in its expression and interpretation are secondary and never a legitimate cause for intolerance and conflict. The world to which our quantum brain links us is whether its wholeness is because of a detailed area within the natural world and even the job of divine transcendent intelligence. To participate in communion with this oneness has been the mission of all spiritual masters and fantastic teachers. To understand the essence of this oneness has been, and is, the final quest of all terrific scientists. Today, physicists seek the one formula that would anchor their well-known "Theory of Everything," the theory that might account for all of the laws of nature and explain things that possibly took place in our integrally entire universe. Einstein stated that understanding this formula will read through the mind of God.

This chapter proves that science and religion are closely interconnected, which makes each of them very interesting. Now, get ready to claim your power with the Akashic Records as you turn to the next chapter!

Chapter 4

Akashic Records and Claiming your Power

"Heal the soul first; then healing of the mind and body will follow"
Zhi Gang Sha

We've probably been through a lot in our past lives, but how much more than our present lives? The only way to move forward is to determine what's been holding you back. In this chapter, you will learn how to become the best version of yourself with the help of your Akashic Records!

Akashic Records Wisdom

Using the Akashic Records has helped me claim my power, break bad habits, and understand myself at a greater level. You can have all of these very same benefits and much more whenever you dive into your Akashic Records. I've been learning about the Akashic Records off and on for years. Each time the subject of Akashic Records came up in my life, I needed it.

Looking back, I was usually at some kind of crossroads or perhaps feeling stuck and wanting to advance.

We're all our unique expressions of living, and the Akashic Records help us to enjoy exactly where we've been.

Growing up, I'd always become mad if my family told me that I was just another family member. I'd often forcefully tell them, that I was not like anyone else! Talk about being strong and independently willed! I did not see the concept of being a family member, since I needed to do things my very own way.

After a reading with a professional, I learned the behavior was a mini expression of one of my divine gifts. My blessing of divine power helps me to become a natural leader, along with an entrepreneur. Having her confirm that helped me to fully stand in my power.

I felt like the well-known square peg trying to slip into the round hole many times in my life. I'm a misfit since I'm here to help bring about change. Using the Akashic Records helped me look back throughout my soul's experiences to confirm it was smart for me to be a leader and to take a stand. I also gained confidence in knowing the sacred actions I'd performed in my other lives. Your soul has already done the job so you can take a few minutes to enjoy how wonderful and unique you are.

Involving myself with my Akashic Records helped me break a lot of unhealthy behaviors. The outer layer of our aura is packed with the energy and experiences from various other lifetimes. This may be an asset to help us pull ancient wisdom into our present lives. But on the other hand, this may be a hindrance when we have problems in need of healing.

The process of rebirth helps us to clear older issues, find out more, and have fun. Based on what's in the outside layer of your aura, you might be unknowingly influenced by those experiences and looking for healing.

If an individual died from starvation in a prior life, they might constantly be overeating and overfilling their pantry. This won't look like a huge deal, but to any person that has been overweight and felt like they couldn't make progress on weight loss, it's a really big deal. When you're armed with the data of your previous lives, you can work through any perceived blocks with ease.

The more you make use of the Akashic Records, the greater you are going to understand yourself. All of us came into this life with divine gifts and intentions about how we would serve others with those gifts. When you do not understand your gifts, how could you work with them to their greatest potential?

When nearly all individuals have their fundamental needs met, why are a lot of people still miserable? The solution is that we've come to a place in our society where individuals are striving for soul satisfaction. Anything under that is unfulfilling. We usually have a choice of how we can carry out our sacred service using our divine gifts. How would you make use of the Akashic Records to unlock your highest potential?

The power of the Akashic Records

The Akashic Records are a vibrational history of each soul's journey from the point of origin. Within the records, all of the experiences throughout each soul's incarnations are taped. Every idea, deed, occasion, word, and emotion has been scribed upon the ethers. Each soul has an Akashic Record, like numerous books, with each book representing one lifetime.

An Akashic Record consultation is simply not like a psychic reading. When your spiritual history is opened, karma and energetic patterns that hold you back can be unblocked. The details in the Akashic Records assist you in the existing moment with what's taking place in your world; within relationships, finances, and what's holding you back. Knowing what energetic patterns are restraining you and what soul lessons you're here to discover can help you navigate life. If you've experienced challenges in relationships, it will be beneficial to learn from the information you're here to discover in this lifetime about relationships. The Akashic Records are precise and can allow you to get in touch with who you are from a divine perspective. Knowing your soul's function in this lifetime is amongst the most typical question asked of the Akashic Records.

Each Akashic Record reading is varied; the questions you appear with alter your reading direction. In a reading with one of my customers, they asked to learn who their guides were. It was important to this male to possess an awareness of his guides, instructors, and masters' names. He'd suspected there to be some extremely crucial and famous beings on his committee. David, in David and Goliath, was one of his guides. This surprised us both!

The Ascended Masters have high vibrational energy, that is of divine love. Finding yourself in the power of the Ascended Masters is powerful and life-changing. Among my clients, were many particularly stubborn and hard-headed, including the following gentleman. He had a few readings over the years but didn't take the information he received to heart. He asked questions to The Ascended Masters and did not make use of the information to initiate changes in his life. In a single reading for this same client, they held back and told him nothing. I had to return his money as I couldn't do his reading. On a subsequent consultation for the same male, the information flowed, and the Masters hit him hard and fast with information, which was quite direct. The Ascended Masters are often loving. However, like a parent, if you do not listen and come back again for subsequent reading, you may be hit with a spiritual two-by-four.

Typically, a customer asks a question, and as soon as they have asked it, the necessary modifications happen. Shining the light of the divine on a subject can alter the course of occasions. In my preliminary Akashic Record consultation, I asked if I was meant to go to Melbourne to study these Akashic Records. I was informed, *"Yes, you're going to Melbourne to study the Akashic Records."* My next question was, "How can I do that when my daughter's wedding event is taking place the same day as the Akashic Records course?" I was informed by the Ascended Masters that I had to speak with my child about her upcoming marital relationship and ask if she still intended on getting married. This was a difficult subject to take up with my daughter; it made her mad with me. I was questioning her power to understand her heart's desire and what was most helpful for her.

However, the result of my discussion with Cara about her wedding event changed the course of history. After our talk, she called me to state they had to customize the date as they did not want their wedding at her fiancé's grandparents' home. As a result, they altered the date to one after I returned from Melbourne, so I was able to attend both my daughter's wedding and the Akashic Records course.

The strength of your story in the Akashic Records

We've all had these moments in the Akashic Records: you understand what you would like to ask, however, you have difficulty phrasing the right question. What is it that I want to know about? Have you experienced this? Or have you experienced this with anybody else that you might have done a reading for?

Here is what I do. Begin to tell your story. Start to share all your experiences, memories, and feelings about what you would like to know and understand. Start at the beginning. Describe just what happened as much as you can recall. The details are great. How did you think about what happened? Explain and share deeply. Keep going with what happened next and how you felt. Keep the focus on you. Keep going until you feel accomplished with most of it.

This particular story-telling is special since it's telling your story. (Or in case you're performing a reading for another person, it's all about them and fully telling them their story without the necessity for you, as the reader, to do anything besides listen, non-judgmentally). It's a time to be a human being experiencing many of our emotions, confusion, angst, truth-telling, and specifically our point of view. When telling your story, you don't have to put in any spiritual thoughts about how the others in the experience truly didn't mean to harm you, or perhaps you know you have to forgive them so that you can heal, etc. Nope! This is all about you in your Akashic Records, so it becomes the story of solely your experience.

As you speak the honesty of your human experience, you might remember long, forgotten details. You may have other memories that seem disconnected that just pop out of your mouth to be shared as well. All of this is okay and better compared to okay; it is great!

What's happening as you do this truth-telling in the space of your Akashic Records, is you start to heal. You're ready to accept the divinely loving and non-judgmental space of your records. You're kept secure and safe in that space. As you tell your story, you start to heal, understand, release, and let go.

It's among the most effective things you can do in your Akashic Records. Tell your story.

I've seen this bring about miraculous release, healing, and understanding with numerous of my clients. In reality, I've had clients who have completely released and reached an innovative understanding of long-standing issues just as they told their story. I've had experiences in my personal Akashic Records, where I discovered a sense of release and relief by telling the story of what happened from my point of view.

Thus, later you have someone ask you a brief question while you're reading through their records, like "why can't I ever be in an excellent happy relationship" and you, as the reader, sit with their Masters, Teachers, and loved ones waiting for the best solution for them, and you ask them to tell the story of what their experience with relationships has been.

Or perhaps later you're feeling stuck about an element of your life, and you believe you cannot get to the bottom serotonin in your personal Akashic Records; so tell your story, from your point of view. Let it be raw. Let it be accurate from your point of view. Let yourself be released because you can, at long last, be completely truthful about your experience in probably the most loving place you could be.

See the wonders that unravel from there!

Have you told your storyline in your Akashic Records without the need to hold the answer first? I'd like to pick up what several of your experiences have been with this powerful and simple tool to utilize in the Akashic Records.

Now you know the power of the Akashic Records! Claim your power and break your bad habits today! If you're curious if you can access the records of others, the answer is yes. The next chapter covers exactly how you can do that!

Chapter 5

Accessing Others' Akashic Records

"All changes, even the most longed for, have their melancholy; for what we leave behind us is a part of ourselves. We must die one life before we can enter another"
Anatole France

Have you ever wanted to access other people's Akashic Records to help them heal from their past? In this chapter, learn how to read the records of others and discover ways on how you can get information from the Akashic Records!

Everybody who ever lived in the world has contributed to the information found within the Akashic Records. For this main reason, everyone can read their personal Akashic Records. The standard to begin a journey in discovering the Akashic Records is having an extremely peaceful outer environment, patience, an open mind, and then you will be all set for an attornment. There's a specific system you can discover before channeling your information, otherwise, you can contact a reader of Akashic Records like me. I've had an attornment myself, and I developed my ability to read through self-reading for a great deal of time.

The individual who wishes to get the reading is invited to ask specific questions on themes that matter to them because the information is a lot of that; it's best to concentrate and choose. Let us remember we're reading a thing that we've created and that we're still writing, a kind of interactive log. Since things are based on free will, it's crucial to ask: ask, and you'll be given.

And who, through the reader, responds to these concerns? Who truly "reads" our register? It's challenging to give a unique response.

For starters, we come into contact with our Higher Self, that's ourselves but with no character, without ego. We manifest our mastery, our spirit, our heart, the divine who's inside us. Many entities are associated with them: Masters of Custody, Ascended Masters, Masters with whom we're resonant, Beings of pure light, Nature of humans that have been near us in this life, Angels, and more.

Sometimes it turns out that our behavior or way of thinking hasn't been acquired in the present life experience but in other lives. In these cases, information is given approximately a single or even more life than the individual has encountered because remembering allows them to let go of what they no longer need.

Calling on various life experiences occurs only when needed for the soul to resolve slopes, but it's not the main objective of reading Akashic Records. You receive information on past life events when you may still find traces in this life that have to be overcome, but frequently you don't need to remember the details; in mind, you understand the origin of the behavior to accept its transformation.

What occurs during a reading? In most instances, the individual who's getting a reading enters an expanded state of consciousness, in which the feeling and time of peace expand.

Sensations and perceptions depend significantly on the receiver's capability to relax. At the same time, those who offer readings must be ready to step aside throughout the process to respect the personal space between the Masters and all those that ask.

An effective reader merely conveys what they perceive, with no interpretation or judgment of what's said, mindful that there's a larger director who selects the information needed for the evolution of the applicant's soul. Therefore, only reveal what a soul must remember at that time.

The recipient of the message resonates with what's said and understands it at a profound level, while also at several levels. It's not simply new cognitive information that enters the thin body of that every single one is composed; the message also impregnates the physical body's cellular memory and brings with it transformation and rebalancing at all levels.

Paradoxically, the brain memory does not constantly hold the information completely, remaining in an expanded state of consciousness, the person typically does not remember what was said throughout the session, so I always suggest recording the reading.

Listening back to your reading at a distance of time is a wonderful possibility to check out new subtleties about the concern. When a connection channel with Akashic signs up is opened during a reading, you will discover great deals of things going on; it's as if we eventually offer the magnificent authorization to run in our power and physical system. The frequency we receive is of the best, it is genuine love that acts in the much deeper levels of our animated memories by providing acceptance and forgiveness.

We receive "karmic healing", consciously renewing episodes of other lives that we have to illuminate in this; we free ourselves from burdens of unsolved situations that we've dragged behind for much too long. And all this happens in the sweetest moving way we can imagine, with the sensation of being spoiled and loved by our ancestors, the angels, the masters who motivate us, from the beings of light we see as a true presence within us.

This sensation of being in a beautiful and big company doesn't leave us anymore. We don't feel truly by ourselves, and we face what we first felt as heavy and difficult, with the heart lightened by the loving touch of our "new" multidimensional friends. That's exactly why I could no doubt point out that contact with the Akashic Records changes life and is the one I witness anytime I look at the Records of others, or when I get the stories of the people who I'd love the opportunity of transmitting the attornment.

By changing our outlook on life, life changes.

Opening our Records begins a self-knowledge work driven by our superior self, the invisible helper, and the heart.

How does it happen? Just how does the information come about? And what's the information? It is love, and it is vibration; it is light.

What I get is much more than words to translate; it transforms within my consciousness at such a pace that it doesn't matter to me, but my mood changes immediately; where there was tension, there's now passion and peace for life.

What information can typically be obtained from you if you open the Akashic Records?

We can find information from the time your soul was created, about your previous lives, present situations, and future possibilities too. It is always revealed to you whatever you have to understand at that moment, at that time, to support you on your journey.

The files are a unique modality. The information is a hundred percent focused on that person whose records are opened, therefore, if you wish to find out about another person, you must first ask for consent to go into their records. Whatever you find out about another person will be through the perception of your record or perhaps your interpretation of that individual. You do not learn about anyone else's soul path.

You can also use the records for business. You can make use of it for a creative process. You can open up the record of an actual space by entering the address instead of the individual's title into the prayer. When you are likely to go in only for yourself, you can ask about career, love, finances, and inspiration. People have used them to write screenplays and books. What you can find out in that space is infinite.

How can you figure out how to flip through the Akashic Records?

Anyone can find out how to flip through the Akashic Records since it's a history of our souls. You don't need to be psychic. The amount and degree of information you get will differ depending on your own personal and special gifts, but everybody has this access. Several individuals are extremely detail-oriented, so perhaps they receive more complex information. Many people see-through color, or they might experience messages through dance or music. But every person has the power to tap into their records.

The records are accessed through a prayer called the Pathway Prayer. The prayer is a vibrational frequency made of specific sounds that permit you to use the Akashic Records. My program demonstrates how to do it through my method. It supplies a good deal more flexibility on guidelines and how you can start delving into the records. When you're in a position to unlock this encyclopedia of assistance, you have it for the remainder of your life. It's like getting a guide in your back pocket. That stated, it might be too intense for some to receive that amount of details.

What's a method of accessing the records?

There's an energetic frequency that goes through our systems. I call it the line, and it originates from the top realm in the universe in which the Akashic Records exist. Through this line, you are receiving messages 24/7. When you detect these messages, it feels like an intuitive hit or an internal knowing. The line is practically an inner filing system that is unique to you. That is the big distinction between dealing with the records. You are not checking out the Akashic Records for other people, however, the messages you get might be about somebody else.

When I began working with the records, I was struggling to put this all together. My record guides told me that my goal is to modernize the Akashic Records to make them easy and accessible. So I teach a free line activation, and people can do it at any time. It is a breathwork and movement practice.

I feel that every person is accessing the data at all times. Even if we're not aware, we're constantly receiving these messages through our souls. Even at our rock bottom, we can pray and gain access to this energy.

Can anyone enter the Akashic Records?

To read the Akashic Record, you have to have Akashic Records Spirit Guides assigned to you - my teacher did it for me through an attunement. It can also happen spontaneously. A well-known intuitive wrote to me saying she would be assigned an Akashic Record Guide spontaneously. This also may occur if you are prepared to use the Hall of Akashic Records on behalf of other individuals. Still, you would need some intuitive ability already to have that happen.

If you wish to have the ability to look up information in the Akashic Records with some degree of accuracy and reliability, I would suggest that you become qualified to do it, as you have to find out which questions to ask and the way to interpret the answers.

So, how can you get information from the Akashic Records?

To go into the Akashic Records, the procedure is comparable to intuitively tuning into someone's Spirit Guides or perhaps Higher-self. The 'tuning in' process' primary element is a visualization that takes you to the Hall of Akashic Records. Nevertheless, after you arrive there, you require Akashic Record Spirit Guides to search for your pertinent information, as the Hall of Akashic Records is a great place. After you're in, you give your guides the relevant birth information, and they locate the best Akashic Record 'file' for you. Next, to check out someone else's 'file' or perhaps soul record, you have to understand what information to search for, and you want a method of retrieving it.

I am not in a trance while I do it, the state that I am in is a similar state an intuitive is in when performing a phone reading for you; living. I'm constantly in a peaceful place when I am reading through the Akashic Records, with no distractions, and I choose to prepare all my readings instead of doing them live, as it is much easier.

Accessing the Akashic Records

To understand exactly why accessing the Akashic Record can be a life-changing experience, imagine you're in a library that extends infinitely in all directions and has books describing all events concerning humanity, both those that have happened and those with people who are anticipated to occur. Anybody who has access to such a library will inevitably be in a position not only to change themselves but also possibly tinker with the course of history.

When you hook up with the Akashic Records, it's said that you'll spiritually elevate yourself to another level. You are going to be ready to recover yourself and others through meditation and secret spiritual rituals. A deep relationship with all living beings will control your soul, and you'll get a brand-new purpose in life. Spiritual masters who have obtained the Akashic Records have discussed gaining a full clarity of idea and deep creativity levels.

As to the issue of where the Akashic Records are, today, that's tricky. The Akashic records don't exist in any physical dimension. Rather, they're located outside the bounds of the typical human understanding of space and time. The records can only be obtained by turning inward, meaning you have to dedicate yourself to intense spiritual cultivation.

The Common Method

Trying to retrieve Akashic Records can be a screening process for some people. They might contemplate for hours on end but never get anywhere near accessing the records. This is amongst the reasons that a lot of curious people eventually stop attempting. Their impatience practically disqualifies them from possessing the data they look for.

You will find numerous methods for accessing Akashic Records. Essentially, you begin by defining precisely what you want to learn. The question has to be certain. When your brain is sharp, and you understand what you're seeking, ask for any spiritual guides to aid you; whether they understand you or not. This should be accomplished when you're in a relaxed, meditative state and are ready to accept suggestions.

When you hook up with every being, ask for their name, and express that you're looking for the files to discover a solution to a certain question. Generally, it takes many attempts to get to the point. Many people get past it and gain access to the Akashic Records, while others fail to do this despite trying several times.

Additionally, individuals with a false experience of Akashic Records hear an authoritative voice that commands them to perform some actions. When you have this, realize that the voice doesn't stand for the Akashic Records. It's highly recommended that one only embarks on their search for Akashic Records under a spiritual master's direction.

Inherent risks

When trying to attempt spiritual techniques, make sure you're spiritually adept. Or else, there could be forces that attempt to interfere, intimidate, and result in damage. When you don't desire to cultivate yourself to a healthy level before attempting some "outreach," you might search for a master to support you. But finding a genuine master who won't con you and use you is hard. They're unusual, and none of the real masters will do such a thing for a reward. They'll just try to teach you a spiritual path that will ensure that you get the capability and knowledge to do what's required on your own.

Astounding insights you can gain if you read a person's akashic record.

The Akashic Records are an etheric place that exists which holds all of our souls' information; past, future, and present. Every person, place, animal, and event has a soul record in the Akashic Records.

When you can read through the records, you're in a position to find out all sorts of information that is interesting about who you are on the soul level - and who others are, too!

In the past, I have covered how we can discover information such as exactly where your soul came from, what you've been doing between lifetimes, what you're learning in this incarnation, and what your primary intuitive gift is through the Akashic Records.

Here, I will discuss other information that we can look up in the Akashic Record.

1. What kind of lifetime is the soul in?

As an Akashic Record reader, it's been apparent to me for some time that as souls, we're all right here on earth in a body for various reasons. Allow me to share several reasons for souls to come here:

Studying Lifetime

Many souls come here to have experiences that change us on the soul level, making it possible for us to grow into new qualities and integrate these into our being.

For instance, a soul chooses to incarnate to learn both perseverance and patience, and it does this by enjoying amazing success. Still, it's the success that will come slowly over time, and success that it has to work hard for (and overcome many difficulties to achieve)!

By the time that life is over, the soul has learned a thing about the energetic qualities of being patient but not quitting, qualities that it is going to take with them into the following incarnations.

A lot of us are in lifetimes in which learning is our main priority on the soul level.

Holiday Lifetime

On the contrary, some souls are here to enjoy themselves and have a great time - no (or very minimal) learning is required.

This usually occurs when the soul has experienced a rigorous series of incarnations. There was a great deal of learning and evolution, therefore, they chose to rejuvenate themselves and gather their energies with a holiday lifetime.

These are typically the sort of lives in which not a great deal from the ordinary happens - the soul tends to incarnate into a loving family, has uneventful relationships, and won't encounter any significant hardships or setbacks.

Contribution Lifetime

This lifetime type is one where the soul will contribute a thing of importance to their neighborhood or even to the community at large. This soul usually feels a strong sense of purpose. Perhaps they're intended to work with a particular group of people, fight for a specific cause, invent something, or even be Prime Minister (to name only a few possibilities).

An individual with this soul will often feel a solid sense of mission and purpose.

Support Lifetime

This is a lifetime in which you're not much a leading man/lady in your personal story, but you are here to have a support role for another person. This means that another individual has lessons they're deciding to study and experiences they wish to experience here. Still, they require you to play a crucial part, to assist them in learning those lessons and having those experiences.

For instance, perhaps you have a disabled child, so the experience of parenting this particular child causes you to develop into a completely different person than you had been before. The soul of that child is apt to have lifetime support, essentially allowing you to have specific experiences you signed up for, even before you got here.

Frequently I find souls select a few of these roles as their priority for any given lifetime. For example, a holiday lifetime plus support lifetime, contribution, and learning lifetime, but some may choose three.

For me, it's been particularly interesting researching the people in my private life as well as finding out the reason they're here.

Additionally, just to clarify that this particular reading component looks into the soul's PRIMARY focus - we do work with all four energies in our lives. For example, just because we're in a 'holiday lifetime' does not mean we will not contribute or perhaps learn anything. And just because we are in a 'learning lifetime' does not mean we will not go through phases of our life where learning slows down and life becomes easier, like a holiday lifetime.

Let us have a look at something else we can discover in the Akashic Records:

2. How many earthly lifetimes has a soul had?

When we read through the Akashic Records, we can ask the number of earthly lifetimes we've had in the whole history of our soul.

This can be exciting and validating - some soul groups usually do not come here often, therefore, at times, the soul can feel 'out of place' here.

Other souls have a long history of being here (some have been coming here for hundreds of years) and also may feel exhausted from this particular location as a result.

I have seen souls with more than one hundred earthly lifetimes under their belts and souls with just a few.

In case you ask this question in the Akashic Records, it's best to bear in mind that the number of earthly lifetimes a soul has had doesn't equate to how evolved that soul is; it doesn't mean anything about the soul's age, or breadth of experience.

This is because all lifetimes are documented in the Akashic Records, regardless of how light they are.

Several souls have tried out a lot of short lifetimes. So ten short earthly lifetimes could, in some cases, be the same as one long one; moreover, it regards what the soul gets to experience.

Additionally, star traveler souls incarnate elsewhere, plus some soul groups are rarely available here at all, while they may incarnate in some other places. We do not understand enough about what those lifetimes are like, whether time even exists there, how evolution occurs, or perhaps even the pace of that evolution. Thus, those lifetimes are often significant too - but they will not show up as earthly incarnations in the person's soul record.

3. Is a person's current career a great fit for their soul's gifts?

I love responding to this question; it is fantastic and the real practical use of the information we can get in the Akashic Records.

When clients ask this, I get a portion of alignment for the client's current job with their soul gifts. We can also get percentages for just about any potential job or career the client is thinking of shifting.

For instance, let us say that my client Hailey is a Mintakan soul (which means she likes to assist others in evolving spiritually, and she's here to take positive, uplifting energies). She's educated in the fourth realm, which corresponds to the heart chakra, so she's a healer too.

Plus, maybe when we look into her many other soul gifts, we discover she's had a past life as a counselor or advisor, and perhaps this is a job she's had on the opposite side too (helping souls to process their most recent lifetime in the life review).

When she tells me that she's been offered work as a debt collections officer, we can understand that this work is just thirty percent aligned with her soul gifts, which signifies that it's not going make use of her soul gifts, so she will be unfulfilled.

Ideally, we're searching for something closer to a hundred percent - a role that allows Hailey to be dealing with individuals on their spiritual evolution and growth; ideally in healing or perhaps a counseling role. When she starts to think about teaching as a psychotherapist, we understand we are now "getting warmer," and we can obtain a percentage and learn specifically what that alignment is. It may be eighty percent aligned, which is better.

Because it is still not the perfect alignment, we can try adding things to the possible career and tweak it (e.g., an equine therapist or a psychotherapist who's also a coach or a therapist working with children), it will then generate a brand-new alignment for every one of those, in a percentage.

Or perhaps it may be Hailey's ideal and aligned career is a blend of two roles.

Essentially, the more often you're using your soul's gifts in your business, the more content you will be, and the more you will add to the world, which often translates to greater prosperity.

Let us have a glimpse at another possible question we can ask in the records:

4. What are the number of previous lives we have shared with another soul, and what kind of lifetimes or relationships were they?

Have you ever met someone and felt like you knew one another in a past life? Perhaps you felt at ease with this particular person immediately, or perhaps you felt drawn to them like a magnet? Perhaps the person evokes a deep emotional response in you, which doesn't feel proportionate, or right for what the relationship is in this lifetime?

In that case, this might be a past life connection. And if you read through the Akashic Records, you can discover the number of times you've come across this soul in the past, as well as what the nature of that relationship was.

For instance, I recently read the soul record belonging to an individual who came into my life and found that we've shared ten lifetimes, particularly as co-workers, and classmates, which helped put the sense I had about this particular person into context.

It's also striking if you run into a soul with who you've been in a romantic relationship for over many lifetimes. Even if you are not intending to have a romantic connection with that soul in this lifetime, you might be ready to feel the echoes of the previous relationships in the current dynamics, and yes, it can produce an unusual amount of familiarity or even intimacy that can feel unsettling and may feel inappropriate. So in scenarios like those, it may be validating to do a little bit of research and discover what you were to one another in the past.

Let us delve into an additional question that I often ask my clients:

5. Has this person had more female or male incarnations?

Many souls show a minimal preference for incarnating as male or female. This just means the soul has much more experience in a male or female body. In several cases, it may feel a great deal more at ease being single-sex over more. This is because historically, there tended to be clear gender roles that we occupied when right here on earth.

For instance, some souls might show up as having been female or male for 75-80% or more of their earthly incarnations. These are the souls who may be susceptible to experiencing gender dysphoria when they come into a body that doesn't match the bulk of their different lifetimes.

It's pretty amazing to know how many lifetimes you've come across a certain person or how many earthly lifetimes we have had. It takes time and patience to learn how to access the records of others and help them heal. Now, how does healing happen within the Akashic Records?

Chapter 6

Healing Within the Akashic Records

"Seek healing, a refilling of energy and spirit, as soon as you see that you need it. You don't have to push yourself to give, do, or perform when what your body, mind, soul and emotions need is to heal"
Melody Bentie

Throughout this book, healing has been a recurring subject. In this chapter, we will discuss exactly how healing happens within the Akashic records.

In contemporary life, nearly all of us do not spend a great deal of time worrying about our soul or how to define it.

Named from the Sanskrit word Akasha, meaning both "sky" and "primal source," the Akashic Records are thought to know all human experience in its entirety through every soul. It's an equivalent concept to the "Book of Life" in the Judeo-Christian tradition.

Instead of thinking of your soul as the thing that endures after you die, consider the innermost part of you that's conscious of itself as divine in nature.

How can accessing Akashic Records heal?

In search of answers, we seek assistance from others looking for a ray of explanation and hope about the sources of what we're going through, as well as a fast solution as a remedy. While the energy field and vibration can provide us some information, the very long-lasting healing power lies deep within our souls.

When Akashic Records are accessed, the information about current life situations is always highlighted. Many times, latent patterns come to the surface to be healed. Akashic Records are like an online supply (if you consider it, they're literally like a virtual library); the more questions we ask, the clearer the answers are that we receive.

Previous life specifics like who I was in the past life or perhaps what I did in that life, isn't essential. What's important is the wisdom that comes from accessing those lifetimes, the insight into any karmic debts, blockages, or perhaps patterns that continue to be manifesting in this life due to previous lifetimes.

The records point out the foundation of such karmic debts, patterns, or blockages, which in many instances can be traced to previous lifetimes. These are associated with unfinished business or pending lessons that the soul has yet to find. In some cases, these are the prompts to remind the soul of lessons mastered in a previous lifetime, waiting to be activated through memory in this lifetime.

Akashic Records provide all of the information and understanding, so one can take appropriate action. They empower us, so we can produce a change in our daily life, release self-limiting beliefs, transform relationships in our outer and inner universe, and embrace peace as a means of living. They never tell us what to do. The counsel comes from a non-judgmental place of compassion and love, providing opportunities for direction and growth for the soul's advancement.

What can they heal?

We can also access lifetimes of trauma from where our fears and phobias are coming from. Clients block these lifetimes out of fear of seeing extremely traumatic or fearful experiences. Sometimes we were perpetrators in a lifetime, where we've harmed people. These require karmic clearance, forgiveness, and healing with all the souls involved; calling upon the soul of the topic. After that, we check for curses or vows from various lifetimes so that all of the curses that are karmically set are dropped. Usually, this involves extensive healing and counseling of the souls involved, with the help of angels and spirit guides.

After the first reading for psychic diagnosis, energy clearance or spirit release therapy is needed to remove foreign energies or spirit attachments, and you will be duly informed in advance. Sometimes black magic also tends to make an individual prone to spirits and health problems, which have to be cleared first.

Will you experience healing by using the Akashic Records?

I have worked for more than ten years to clear the feelings of abandonment and unworthiness magnified by losing two childhood friends. If you, like many people, are considering the Akashic Records, your reaction may be, "Ten years!! I thought the Akashic Records had been a shortcut to healing!"

The fact is they are. Without them, I would not have released anywhere near the amount of karma and past life experiences that kept me wrapped in pain. Healing often works in a spiral. As you grow, brand new levels of information come up to be healed, understood, and seen. That translates to ten days more than ten years.

Had I not spent those ten years guided to awareness by the Akashic Masters, I definitely could not live the life I have today; filled with love, trust, and curiosity. I'd most probably be by myself, making a great deal of money but suffering in unimaginable ways.

In my work with the Akashic Masters, they have shared that many of us have lived more than three hundred lives right here on Earth. Consider the thousands of experiences, each one a small pebble, causing ripples in the energy field of your soul! Layer upon layer of physical and emotional memories surround you, usually causing pain in both your body and mind.

Any damage or mental pain you have brought along with you into this life is kept in the etheric level of your aura; the one closest to the actual physical body. This layer contains electric energy pathways that provide life force for the physical body and are home to emotions you do not consciously remember. These long-forgotten memories continue to result in blockages and subtle disturbances until they go into the denser physical body displaying illness, disease, and pain.

Because this energy has different layers, each is created by its own experience. The sole method to heal is to remove them one by one. This happens as we're prepared to look at and also understand the effect on our present life. We then process and incorporate the information into our lives; it enables us to be prepared for a brand-new layer to arise for healing. The energy then rises as a spiral as we heal the different layers.

To me, it is magic that it has just taken ten years to clear what I brought with me from other lives, old relationships, and previous experiences to produce the life I have now. While it might look like a while, I can't fathom how life would be, had I not begun the journey.

My connection with the Akashic Masters has given me the information I needed to identify and let go of the old experiences that kept me bound in pain.

Connect with your Akashic guides and take the next phase in freeing yourself from anything rooted in your past, which causes you pain!

In conclusion, it's important to clear yourself of all the karmic energy your past life has brought you. It's the only way to heal and move forward with your life. In the next chapter, you will discover how to use the Akashic Records to heal yourself.

Chapter 7

Using the Akashic Records to Heal Yourself

"The soul always knows what to do to heal itself. The challenge is to silence the mind"
Caroline Myss

Now that we understand how healing happens within the Akashic Records, let's go deeper into how to use it to heal yourself. In this chapter, learn the basic techniques to heal from your past life!

The Akashic Records will be the deepest healing tool kit that we all have access to, healing your mind, soul, and body, as well as your heart from deep-seated wounds.

It reveals the blind spots you might not be prepared to discover, and the most profound part is that you're removing subconscious programming that no longer benefits you. This is an automatic quantum leap to your soul's journey.

This is a tool for receiving probably the deepest healing, as you're in a position to heal relationships with your partner, friends, family, yourself, money, and whatever else you discover you have a total block with; resulting in recovery on a physical, emotional, mental, spiritual, and dynamic level.

Akashic Records will be the solution to your soul and heart. By delving into your heart versus your head, you're accessing the universal truth of the deepest part of your being. Your heart lets you feel your feelings, allowing you to heal and resulting in a big shift in your actions.

Imagine that you are wearing a raggedy coat that's heavy and old, this is the subconscious programming you've created since you have been born. The Akashic Records allows you to eliminate this raggedy coat so can be the real essence of who you are; gaining clarity on your soul's purpose, as well as your talents and gifts.

Ten ways the Akashic Records can heal your life

Are you having one of *those* months? Or worse yet, one of *those* years? Only when you thought you had your life all figured out, everything comes crumbling down. You're feeling like a fighter down for the count, and the Universe keeps punching. Why is this happening? You have been working hard on yourself, trying to follow an enlightened life. So why is it all so messed up? Well, it's because the Universe has greater plans for you, and it is all tied in with your Akashic Records.

As lightworkers, we come into this existence intending to achieve a lot of things. But perhaps the most powerful lightworkers can get swept up in the minutiae of living and forget about the big plans that have been made for your soul. This is when the Universe jumps in. When you are not progressing as planned, the Universe starts sending you messages. Little, in the beginning, a message may merely be a sensation of discontent with your job. In case you ignore this particular message, you will get a bigger one. Perhaps you will meet up with someone doing precisely what you love to do, and you have a quick rush of excitement as well as envy.

Fortunately for us, the Universe is quite persistent. In case you ignore that first signal, the Universe takes the following (and bigger) step. You lose your job.

What initially feels like a huge hit is a big hint. You had taken a detour, and so it is time to get back on track. You got the message because of the Universe.

By opening your Akashic Records, you retrieve information about the plans you made coming into this life, the lessons you planned to learn, any karma, contracts, or vows you brought from previous lives, and guidance to show that you're progressing the quick way.

Listed here are the foremost reasons you need to pay attention to the wisdom of the Akashic Records:

One) For life answers

Your Akashic Records hold all of the information from all of your lives. The beings and the information of light that keep your records are here to support you. They're able to assist you with small tasks like organizing your week or even major decisions like, "Is this the person I am supposed to marry? Do we have soul agreements to support each other? Do we have old lessons or karma to learn?" Where else are you able to ask these kinds of questions and know the answers will be there?

Two) Clear negative beliefs

Akashic Records enable you to look at the core beliefs that create recurring issues in your life. Some limiting patterns and beliefs come from previous lives, some from your current life.

You can dig into these situations and beliefs, causing you to feel unworthy and clear and unsatisfied at an Akashic level.

Three) Create amazing changes

Have you been looking to possess a true aha moment so you can feel in your heart the truth behind a situation? Your Akashic Records can provide you with the clarity you need to choose to move ahead in a relationship, a career change, or any other important situations in your life.

Four) Your soul's wisdom

Your soul has strengths and talents. By learning about them, you can make strong choices and decisions to align with who you are as an ancient and wise soul. Your Akashic Beings of Light hold the information that will help you understand and believe the truth behind who you are.

Five) Countless possibilities

Your Akashic Records can help you understand that you have more choices out there than you may think. You can check out those choices with your Akashic Masters and receive validation about the best and highest options for your soul today. You can also learn how your present choices are affecting you and what new choices will be like.

Six) Spiritual guidance

For nearly all people to create a change, we must validate that the possible change is a great idea. Your Akashic Records can give you your very own soul-level perspective, which will enable you to have the ability to make the changes that you like.

Seven) Realign your energy.

The Akashic Records are a part of divine source energy; probably the highest vibration available. By accessing your personal Akashic Records, you can achieve an amazing energetic clearing of any restrictions and blocks found there. Through deep work, you can restore your alignments to divine love, abundance, truth, light, and strength.

Eight) An inner strength

In case you are prepared to make a real change, you must realize that change comes from consistent work and commitment and the complete willingness to change. Your Akashic Beings of Light are here to help and support you every day in walking your path to change.

Nine) Past life understanding

People talk about finding a real soul and purpose path. By connecting with your Akashic Records, you can find out about your soul lineage as well as the great lives you have lived. These effective, great lives are what we bring to this life to share and experience. When you understand who you are at the soul level, you might become clear and firm in your commitments and decisions to be on your soul path.

Ten) Feel connected

Through your records, you will experience a profound connection with who you are as a soul and your connection to the divine source of the Universe. You are going to experience a profound sensation of peace and joy in knowing we're all One.

Healing at a soul level

In case you've been attempting to manifest a thing in your life that you're not attracting, and if you are focusing on your long term, then you could be heading down the wrong path.

Sometimes, it is often something from your past that is holding you back.

It may seem contrary to conjure up the past, particularly an uncomfortable memory, to make a happier future. Are you not looking forward to putting all that behind you? If it was hard, why bring it up now? Are you not done with that already? (Especially after all of the self-help you have already done!) Nevertheless, healing your past can typically be the fastest path to creating a happy future.

I see this all the time. A client visits doctors, therapists, and healers with very little change in their lifetime. They do affirmations and create vision boards, but all remain static.

Usually, there's a design from their childhood or a past life that is preventing them from getting what they desire. For example, if somebody wishes to look for their soul mate and observes their parents in an unhappy marriage, they may have a subconscious fear that being married means misery.

Or perhaps, a person who wishes to be pregnant now who died in childbirth in their past life could have a subconscious fear about going into labor. The beauty of discovering and healing your past patterns can completely liberate you to make a joyous, fulfilling future.

Akashic Records are part of you.

The memories of your past, such as your past lives, are saved in your energy, body, subconscious, and the Akashic Records. In the Akashic Records, the present, your past, and future are all connected. Thus, whenever you heal the energy from your past, you're healing everything in both the past and present.

You do not require any special powers to use your Akashic Records since they are a part of you. With sincere inquiry, prayer, and meditation, you are going to be ready to tune in to all you have to know to support you. The Akashic Records are infinite, so you won't ever run out of resources!

Basic Techniques

Here's an easy technique you can use right now:

- Start by sitting quietly and calm your brain. If you're acquainted with meditation, spend a little time in meditation.
- Say a prayer to hook up with your angels and High-level Spirit Guides to aid you, as well as ask for you to be connected only with light.
- Write down, think, or perhaps say aloud what you wish to know much more about. For instance, think of energy you want to heal. You can ask your guides and angels to help you gain insight into the energy foundation from any lifetime.
- Ask what lessons you have to know from experiencing this.
- Ask for forgiveness for all of the individuals involved, and let that energy go.
- Imagine what you'd love to experience. Allow yourself to be filled with light, love, and that healing frequency.
- Spend some time journaling, integrating, and reflecting on your brand-new energy. You are going to feel different!

To conclude this chapter, keep in mind that you must meditate once in a while to connect deeper with yourself. Knowing yourself and your past will be your gateway to healing. Let's dig deeper into healing our past lives!

Chapter 8

Healing Past Lives in the Akashic Records

"We do not heal the past by dwelling there; we heal the past by living fully in the present"
Marianne Williamson

The significance of our past life to our present is endlessly discussed in the past chapters. What exactly is their role in our present life? In this chapter, you'll learn extensively about healing past lives in the Akashic Records.

You have had lives before this one; hundreds, possibly even thousands. And you have brought memories of your past life into this one.

You have likely had them show up in your dreams. Perhaps you have had split-second' flashbacks' in which you feel as you are in two places simultaneously. (Have you ever thought about Dejà Vu as past life memories?) These memories can influence your desires, emotional responses, and fears. They may be the main reason you hold things that are certain to be real without actually knowing why.

Even if you have lived thousands of previous lives, you will just have the ability to recall some in this life. Why? Because the ones you have brought with you are here to educate you on your soul's journey and goal.

Some bring patterns, behaviors, traumas, or memories to release. Some bring reminders of your best strengths and capabilities. And some you bring forward to just experience once again for greater learning.

How would you define a past life?

I prefer the phrase "alternate lifetime" to refer to previous lives. Time and space cease to exist if you start exploring psychic dimensions. Rather, we perceive multiple dimensions of reality where all versions of ourselves are happening simultaneously. From this perspective, our existence isn't linear. We don't disperse our identity on a timeline that initiates at birth and concludes at death. Our souls have cyclical lives, like an infinity sign that folds over itself. But there's a place in everybody's energy field called the Akashic Records, holding their entire soul's history; past, future, present, parallel. Thus, through these records, we're in a position to use some moments within a soul's journey.

Exactly how can our past life help us heal the soul?

I use the Akashic Records in my healing work to remove past lives that could carry lower vibrations, imprints, and stuck energy that is inhibiting a soul's evolution. A past life wound may show up as a karmic illness due to energy that has been leftover from another lifetime, which occurs today to balance or complete karma for an individual. When utilized as an opportunity for metamorphosis, karmic illness has the potential to alter an individual's path in life for their best benefit. I make use of past lives to help create resolution and context through self-awareness. The basic act of acknowledging a past life through reading has the potential to alleviate karma. Almost any time our consciousness expands in this way, we increase our potential for evolution.

Can it be feasible for past life or perhaps a parallel life to affect our current life? How?

Yes. This is the nature of the universe. Everything is connected, and everything is occurring simultaneously. Your present life can also influence your past life or alternate life for the very same reason: everything is occurring simultaneously. That's the reason it's important to be conscious and present about the decisions you are making and how you're making them. Otherwise, you might be creating karma for yourself in some other existences. At any time, you have the option to live from a higher vibration, to evolve in a way. Opportunities are usually showing up in the present moment for you to pick a higher vibration and find out your lesson. In case we decide to resist, we make problems for ourselves because we are simply not evolving as we ought to be.

Past lives now guide us to the Akashic Records

This brings us to the Akashic Records, exactly where all of this was and will be, is stored - along with past lives.

Psychics believe that there's a place where every human word and deed throughout all time has been recorded. Those records are a set of every human event, intent, emotion, word, or thought that has happened in the past, present, or future, and they are known as the Akashic Records. This repository of information of human consciousness is encoded in a non-physical existence known as the etheric plane.

This library of all existence holds the record of your soul's journey from the very first time you emerged into the source until you ultimately return home. Whether or not you're a brand-new soul or an old one, the Akashic energy is the holographic repository of all your thoughts, feelings, deeds, and actions from each lifetime you've previously lived in.

Just knowing who you remained in the past, who you are today, and who you are indicated to have in your future affects the life you lead now. It affects your relationships, your belief systems, and the future truths you draw toward yourself.

Who can access the Akashic Records?

Everyone can access the details from the Akashic Records at any time and from anywhere. The flashes of intuition and understanding hunches that take place every day are a peek of the Akashic Records' knowledge. Everyone in the Universe contributes to and can access the Akashic Records because we're all developed by and plugged into its energy. Our magnificent bequest includes having an opportunity to access the knowledge contained therein.

It's likely to discover your relationships, your health, your soul path, even your past lives, and each conceivable alternate topic. During an Akashic reading, the responses you get offer help and hope, and empowerment by knowing the truth of your circumstances and the possibilities unfolding in your life.

Just how can I access the Akashic Records?

How can you gain access to this information? It is very simple. You relax and start with an open mind. You take on the stance that it's possible. It's all about surrounding yourself with the most loving and healing energy you can muster.

It's vital that you feel truly secure in a zone of benign emotions and achieve a trance-like state. Should you feel rushed or uncertain about your results, it will be hard to retrieve the information you seek. Take the time to focus on what you might need and proceed with confidence. Here are a few formal steps to enable you further:

- Discern what you wish to learn. Be concise and clear. For instance, "I intend to travel to and access the Akashic Records."
- Ease your mind, be in a meditative space. Put together an agreement with your subconscious self that you will come to each of the day's to-dos later on. Focus on your purpose of accessing the Akashic Records.
- If you're working with guides, ask for their assistance now.
- State your specific question out loud. Be precise, concise, and clear with your question. All questions are okay. You might say, "I'd love to find out what's appropriate for me to know about my most recent past life." Be patient as the answer comes.
- Use your senses: sight, touch, taste, sound, feeling, and smell. Who's it connecting with you? Ask this spiritual being to come forward. Ask their name. Next, listen as they react to your question. Your answer could be available in song, a sound, a symbol, an image, a memory, or perhaps a feeling. Once again, pay very close observation to all of your senses, even your physical body.
- As you prepare to finish, thank the spiritual presence for sharing their message. Today, make an effort to journal this experience. Did you get your answer? Did you access the Akashic Records? What did it feel like? Did you see structures? It could be that you saw domes or temples. Maybe you were led to scrolls or a library?

Everyone is going to have a distinctive experience. You might come across spirit guides or angelic-like forms. If beyond doubt, this experience is comparable to channeling, and you might feel as if you are in a dream. Did you feel as you were in a movie? This is feasible as you prepare to accept the sacred documents of all that is, actually was, or ever will be. Whatever your experience, it's real and sacred. You can access this anytime you wish.

Remembering past-lives

The Akashic Records keep the memory of your soul's past, including respective life lessons and past lives. I am in a position to draw on the Records of anyone in an easy-to-use way.

I will go through several of the things I have learned regarding past lives and their healing. Past lives aren't the only thing that can be read in the Akashic Records, but it is surely a topic that many people can reference, given there is a fair amount of coverage about it in some mystic traditions.

For starters, this particular topic is usually a catalyst for people to peek into just how things work in a religious sense. While past lives are dealt with by several religions, they are cultural or religious themselves; it is how the "system" is set up.

People repeatedly incarnate for the goal of their soul's lessons. Temporarily experiencing a good level of focus and limitation allows consciousness to explore itself in great detail, in a manner that would normally never be possible.

The next element that I have learned, in a general sense, is that past lives can help you if you give them the chance.

In a single person's life, she was a wife in a harem in North Africa, and she wanted the love of her husband all for herself. Nevertheless, regardless of how much she fought for it, she never could quite reach it because her husband had a harem. In this life, she's meant to learn to just take the love that loves her back the way she wants to.

Thirdly, your past lives aren't intended to affect the way you run your life today or dictate your mood. If you have "hot buttons" - things you're extremely vulnerable to where once another person pushes them you flip and react very emotionally, then you might have an unresolved issue within a past life. That is usually the case.

When someone triggers your buttons the memory is stimulated, and at that moment, it is like it's your past life character, without you present, is responding to the circumstances. You're "out of yourself." Additionally, it would mean that such an issue could be tackled by recovering the past life, understanding exactly how it relates to you, and what you might learn from it.

If, like the great majority of people, you have had a huge selection of past lives, or perhaps more, then several of them are possibly more productive than others, based on what you decided to experience in this life.

You don't have to know your past lives. They're only significant if they contribute to something within your current moment in a positive sense. Because truthfully, it is just your present moment that counts to you. It is only your present focus of attention that matters. That is what your Spirit wants, for you to know what it wants you to do and wherever it wants to go next.

Nevertheless, accessing your past lives, however you do this, always has the goal of healing and broadening your spiritual knowledge; both overall and about yourself.

Digging deeper into our past lives makes us more conscious and aware of the present. Knowing about it greatly helps in our process of healing. In the next chapter, learn how meditation helps us connect with our Akashic Records.

Chapter 9

Meditation and the Akashic Records

"Do not dwell on the past, do not dream about the future, concentrate the mind on the present moment"
Buddha

I've mentioned before that you can access your Akashic Records through meditation. In this chapter, learn the different types of meditation and how to properly execute them to achieve a deeper connection with yourself and a successful journey to the Akashic Records.

I've had the good fortune to have too many great teachers who have pointed out how to understand meditation.

I recall the very first one, a Zen Buddhist teacher (Sensei). When I was only nineteen years of age, during meditation, he used to stroll around where we had been sitting, checking to ensure we had the best posture and we didn't move. He used to have a branch with him, and the moment I moved, he would hit me with the branch whilst saying, "Do not move.".

Well, I got whacked with that branch typically since I couldn't keep still, my foot would go to sleep, my leg would go numb, my ear would itch; I think you can relate to this. Finally, I told him, "Sensei, I come here to practice meditation, and you keep whacking me with the branch."

He informed me, "You do not belong here, vanish."

Wow! What a statement to make to a nineteen-year-old who knew nothing about meditation. I waited in his presence while I was processing this declaration because, in truth, I did not want to go away. He saw this and said to me, "Go home and sit for thirty minutes without any moving, if you can do that, return once again." So, I did. I went home, started practicing, and finally, after a couple of weeks, I managed to take a seat for half an hour without moving.

I more than happy went to him and told him, "Okay, I can do it now."

He looked at me and said, "Okay, go home and return when you can sit for fifty minutes."

I accepted the challenge, and without question, I went home and started practicing until I could sit for fifty to sixty minutes.

I went back and told him, "Okay, I am capable of doing it now!" Without saying one word, he pointed me towards a cushion, and I sat to meditate.

After the meditation, he stated to me, "You will never have the ability to control your mind without first mastering your body." That was the gem, the treasure that he provided me with that has stayed with me for most of my life.

So how can the Akashic Records play out in meditation? Suppose we realize that the Akashic Fields are unlimited and vast, a very subtle vibrational frequency that exists everywhere around in the past. In that case, it's contained in the present and will continue with no limitations into the common future.

In 2014, Quantum Physicists acknowledged this field and named it the Akashic Field, a niche that is continuously affected by anything alive. The field's performance normally records those imprints or effects, so it's continuously receiving from nature, from components, animals, the world, people, and our mental bodies.

The Akashic Records are unlimited energy fields; they're called Akashic since they're composed of Akasha, meaning primary or energetic substance, the substance from which all life is formed. The goal of the fields would be to record all of life's experiences. The Akashic Records contain present and past knowledge, expressions, and experiences of the soul's journey from its beginning, in addition to the chance of the unfolding of future events. Akasha is everywhere; it's the connective tissue that keeps the universe together, similar to the connective tissue in our very own bodies.

The Akasha is the primordial domain of the cosmos, the domain that hooks up and remembers. Everything that happens in time and space is subtly connected with the rest, and everything that happens remains in space and time; it's saved similarly to items entered on the cloud and the internet. Akasha is the cosmic internet that keeps a record of all things in the Universe.

The presence of a deep domain of the world beyond the domain we experience looks like a subjective insight, beyond objective reality. Yet, it's an insight that has been widely talked about in the historical past of thought. Plato called it the Realm of Ideas and Forms and recognized it as the Seat of the Soul.

The Hindu Rishis called Akasha the complete truth; the supreme truth of the world, eternal and eternally imperishable, changing and molding our universe. The world of time and space is Lila, the unceasing play of disappearance and appearance, forming and dissolution. It is but a symptom of Akasha.

It is said that Akasha is an all-penetrating existence. It has form, all of the things that are the outcome of the combination are developed out of Akasha. Paramahansa Yogananda stated that the Akasha is the subtle background against which all things start to be perceptible. What about an equivalent viewpoint by the famed physicist David Bohm, who noted that the real meaning of things might be seen just when we consider that they arose from an underlying field. He called the area the implicate order.

And so, our soul and its evolution from the second of our soul's formation to this very moment, one lifetime after another, we've left behind an imprint of all our interactions and actions with life itself.

The effect is a library of memories saved on this field; we can call our personal Akashic Records; the Book of Life. So they go from the very personal to the broadened version of interactions that we have with others, let's say our family, and the shared karma from one life after another; in this case, we have communal records. We have cultural Akashic Records, a group of people, and a tribe that is evolving at their very own speed as a lifestyle, maintaining a tight karmic bond between them. We can then make it bigger than that and go to planetary Akashic Records and go from there to universal records and go to infinity.

So, consider the potential to explore outer and inner worlds or fields if we're in a position to connect or even go into these fields and scrutinize. We can do our meditations with our Akashic Records open and have our meditation practice take a greater meaning. If we would like to examine the state of our head and its link to our emotions, then being inside of the Akashic Fields and our private Book of Life is likely to make it easier to use the root cause, or the moment of inception of that emotion, since it might not be the very first time we experience that particular emotion. We can then explore the fields until we discover the first time we experienced that emotion and heal it.

So, no matter the kind of meditation you do, the Akashic Records can provide you with a much greater experience. A few years back, I was in the presence of one of my Gurus, and I asked him something about my meditation; I asked him about the major points of meditation. He asked what sort of meditation I was doing, and I told him mindfulness of breathing. "What will you focus on when you stop breathing?" he asked. I thought it was a beautiful question, and in several seconds, I managed to understand the emptiness that I generated when I stopped breathing. I started then giving the same amount of attention to the inhale and hold, then exhale and hold.

Mantras and contemplative prayers are other types of meditation. These can be described as pure undivided attention while chanting or perhaps praying. This is what all contemplative practices have in common; a thread that connects them all and that may be woven in a wide range of skillful directions based on the purpose and direction we give them. There are many meditation methods. Others focus on the field of perception itself, and we call those methods mindfulness; others focus on a certain object, and we call those concentrative practices. Additionally, some techniques shift back and forth between the object as well as the area.

Meditation, simply defined, is a better way of being aware. It's the happy coming together of being and doing, like both sides of a bridge. When we have the patience to sit and look, little by little the muddy waters of the mind, the chattering which feels ever-present in our mind comes to a stop, and we're then in a position to find out what hidden behind it; slowly we can release the brain as well as the heart. This moves us from thought or emotion to experience an unusual reality that gives us understanding and clarity.

Meditation masters teach many different things about meditation. One of the key things they talk about is to be completely contained in this one breath, this particular moment, not the future or the past but the now; we can call this a transcendental moment of the nowness. In Akasha's field, this is the eternal dimension of its classic presence, vertical or horizontal, where there is no linear time but past, present, and the chance of the future in the now. Many people have difficulty being contained in the now, but exactly where else could they be? It isn't at this exact moment. Meditation is a better way of being present and recognizing who we are.

How about meditation posture?

Different schools recommend different postures; several of them emphasize a still, erect, and formal posture. Others are much more adaptable and more focused on internal movements. But both focus deeply on conscious internal movements.

The Buddhist and other traditions suggest an upright, erect spine, hands relaxed on the lap, with the belly soft, the shoulders rested, the chin slightly tucked in, the jaw relaxed, the tongue behind the top of the teeth, and the legs crossed in the lotus position. You must have an erect spine because this way, the light, energy, and energetic flow can go from the foundation of the backbone to the crown and back again undisrupted. If you're unable to sit cross-legged on the floor, sitting on a chair assuming a similar erect position will be okay.

In His teachings, Buddha gave us four postures to meditate: lying, walking, standing, and sitting down. In case you consider it, this is fairly simple: whenever you sit, you know you're sitting; whenever you stand, you know you're standing; when you're walking, you know you're walking, whenever you're lying down, you know that's what you're doing. Out of all these, lying down to me isn't as helpful because there's the natural tendency to fall asleep.

Learn to sit down as Buddha, stand like Buddha, walk like Buddha. Be as Buddha; this is the primary point of Buddhist practice.

Buddha enlightened six types of meditations: number one, which to me is most critical of all, is analytical meditation. This is an effective meditation in which you're analyzing your emotions and the connection between them and your brain's state. If we experience one predominant emotion, let's say anger, we can meditate on that anger from the present to the past in our lives. In case we understand how to use our Akashic Records, then more power is provided to the process since we can enter the Akashic Fields and explore from present to past, as well as search for the second of the formation of that anger in our lives. The main cause can be from this life or a past life and this is the beauty of Akasha; it might take us to the moment we gave birth to that emotion, allowing us to understand it and heal it. Let's remember that every thought, action, energy exchange, and emotion we've previously experienced is recorded in our private Book of Life in the Akasha.

This particular meditation is exactly what I call the means of self-freedom from the chains that chain us to negative emotions and beliefs that do not serve us in our lives. When we're clear of that, we can move with greater ease into the future.

The next type is a meditation of love, in which you need to change your heart to that frequency. Adjust your heart and wish it far more for others than for yourself, wishing for the wealth and welfare of all beings, like the happiness and bliss of your enemies, wish for them to achieve more love in their life so that they're in a position to contain. Go from the current to the past, review all your relationships, bring each person into your head, wish them and give them love. Eventually, you will think about your father and mother and wish them so much love and appreciation for their presence in your life.

Another type of meditation is the meditation of compassion. You believe and imagine all beings in distress, as clearly as you can, feeling their anxieties and sorrows arise deep compassion in your soul. How's compassion different than pity? Pity is feeling sorry for someone, perhaps you see a beggar in the street, and you say, "Oh poor man, I feel sorry for him," sorry energy isn't compassion. Compassion is the genuine and true feeling for others to be clear of suffering and pain and wish them to be free and happy. So, you might wish to notice and say in your meditation the following:

- May all beings obtain joy and happiness.
- May all remain clear of sadness and the causes of grief.
- May all never be detached from authentic happiness.
- May all remain in a state of calmness devoid of aversion and accessories.

The fourth type is a meditation of joy, where you think of the health, of rejoicing, and others with their rejoicing. Suppose you've already had any kind of friendship or relationship that has come to an end, and that end wasn't joyous. If that's the situation, you can use this meditation to change the Akashic imprints left by your actions on your field and another person's area. So, you're likely to bring that person to your mind's eye and see them shining and smiling in their best light with lots of pleasure in their lives. You can discuss all of your interactions in this same way.

The fifth type is a meditation on the impurity in which you think about the consequences of wrongdoings or the evil effects of corruption; you might want to think about how simple the joys of a moment are and just how long and fatal the consequences are. Think about karmic imprints in the Akashic Fields and how you're entangling yourself at a karmic level with another person or perhaps with a team. In your meditation and with your Akashic Records open, you can return to the moment in which the wrongdoing or even the entanglement was created. There you are going to be in a position to find out the action you had taken and the psychological damage you created in yourself and also the various others. The action can't ever be undone, but the emotional imprint can easily be undone and healed by simply connecting with yourself, and with consciousness, you can ask for forgiveness.

The sixth type of meditation is a meditation on serenity. In this kind of meditation, you want to develop the sensation of internal peace that you wish to raise above hate and love. You wish to forget about all your wants, all of the stagnated emotions, you would like to forget about the constant chattering of the mind, and just rest in the feeling, the sensation of inner peace and serenity.

In case you recognize the way to use your Akashic Records, all of this will require a brand-new flavor. Your meditations will be sweeter, a lot deeper, and more significant as you explore the outer and inner worlds and you blend your whole reality into the oneness of being; leaving behind the feeling and all struggle of separation from the source.

May your meditations be beautiful and sweet, may you have the ability to infuse them with love, empathy, and kindness for yourself and others, and may your mind find internal peace.

The real difference between meditation as well as the Akashic Records

This question speaks straight to how meditation and operating in the Akashic Records are similar or different.

In meditation, the focus is to point you to a place in which you let go of your brain's exercise. Meditation is trying to allow yourself to calm the frantic parts of your head and your being, helping you to discover the peace of balance within you.

However, the point of concentration in the Akashic Records is to enable you to step out of the frantic part of your brain. But it's not asking you for the awareness to be quiet. To focus on the Akashic Records would be to be concerned about the dynamic activity within the flow of knowledge within the Records.

This lively activity can be transmitted in several ways, including sound, touch, feeling, sight, and taste. The concentration brings you into a pinpoint awareness of the lively expression of the Akashic Records' motion and knowledge through you. There is peace and balance there, but it is not silent like meditation.

From a dynamic perspective, meditation helps you stroll into the flow's peace, whereas working the Akashic Records helps you enter the circulation's expression.

When you walk into the Akashic Records, you are asking yourself to concentrate on the flow of knowledge as it is conveyed through the peace and balance of light and sound. In contrast, meditation asks your concentration to take you to a peaceful, balanced, quiet place.

When you remain in the Akashic Records, you might be mindful of all of the tense things that are going on in your very own mind. However, instead you are finding out how to bring your focus of awareness to the movement of knowledge in that moment within peace and balance. Still, you are presently mindful in a way that you are not when you are practicing meditation.

I find meditation a benefit when I am in my Records, as I am already in that relaxed state. My focus is clear, positive, and continuous. I work in my Records and lose my sense of time. Meditation is similar, as essentially, you have lost the understanding of exactly how time is passing.

Operating in the Akashic Records is an active form of meditation, but it is unique. The purpose or objective of the Akashic Records is different. The difference remains in conscious awareness. With time, my Records experience has assisted me in quieting those frantic parts of my brain.

Is it advisable to meditate or even open your Akashic Records? Like many, it is not the question to ask. Rather, what is going to serve me in this particular moment? At times, it'll be meditation; other times, it's exploring the Akashic Records.

Your truth is your path. And how you get to your truth is your choice.

Meditation really benefits your mind, body, and soul. It helps you focus and concentrate better. In the next chapter, you'll learn thoroughly about reading the Akashic Records.

Chapter 10

Reading the Akashic Records

*"Suffering is due to our disconnection with the inner soul.
Meditation is establishing that connection"*
Amit Ray

In this chapter, you'll learn some sample questions you can ask while reading your Akashic Records. You might think that whatever question you ask will have an answer, but the truth is that it depends on how you ask them.

Do you desire to have a deeper understanding of exactly why you're here as well as your objective on this planet?

The Akashic Records are the active records of sentient beings and all the souls who imprint information about their existence.

Your personal Akashic Records holds information about your previous lives, potential future lives, and present life.

These files can be accessed so that you can learn the divine information about your lessons and life purpose when you're prepared.

The information is only one element of the picture; when you learn the information from your Akashic Records, you transcend the experience.

This shifts the record itself so that you can produce a greater vibration.

When you have a Reading in the Akashic Records, you see your life from another viewpoint, and you heal your past; your change is great.

Since these readings are from the Quantum Field of all possibilities, you unfold your soul's essence and find covert skills and abilities.

The most thrilling part of Akashic Record reading is that you can ask questions ranging from the usual to the greater and more religious!

You can ask about your finances or perhaps relationship patterns, your health, past lives, or past traumas; it's as unlimited as the Akashic Records are!

You can also dig deeper into your soul's purpose or your vibration, as well as your spiritual essence or perhaps esoteric information.

Akashic Record Readings will be the most effective information you can access that will enable you to shift your vibration and consciousness to be the reality of all you are!

Customers frequently ask me for sample questions to ask during an Akashic Records reading. Asking great, open-ended, self-focused questions will take your reading to a greater level. In this book, I provide context about what the Akashic Records are, how they work, what to anticipate from a reading, plus twenty-eight sample questions to ask your Records.

What are Akashic Record readings? What can I expect from them?

I occasionally refer to this kind of reading as a "soul reading" - which is easier and convenient for many people to realize. Just as with Tarot or other religious systems, Akashic Records reading will be the same.

Some readings are solely about your past life encounters. Other readings are more centered on the present and/or possibilities for the future. Other readings can focus on a broad range of issues as well as topics, including (but not limited to):

- How you can hook up with your Spirit Guides more clearly
- How you can work with your intuition
- The way to release limiting behaviors and beliefs
- Whether current patterns and habits originate in a past life (and why/how)
- Whether you have made any past life contracts with someone who you know in your present life
- How you can release unhelpful past life vows (such as vows of obedience, self-punishment, suffering, poverty, and so on)
- How you can heal old wounds and traumas

Preparing for an Akashic Records reading

I do not ask for a lot of preparation before performing a reading in my work with clients. I ask my clients to think of approximately two to three pressing questions or issues they'd love to explore together. Nevertheless, I do not want to understand their questions in advance, which might make me consider the reading ahead of time. I would rather begin the reading as fresh as I possibly can so I can easily allow the most relevant information and energy to come through at that moment, without any preconceived agendas or ideas.

You need to be open and receptive before you come to your reading or session. This simply means trying to clear your mind one day or even several hours before the reading. Meditate, pray, do yoga, write in your journal, eat clean food, do not drink alcohol, do not watch the news - whatever works to clear your head and open your heart to the information you want to receive.

Do not be nervous about receiving specific information about your work, life purpose, marriage, relationship, or perhaps other questions you pose. Getting information about something does not mean you have to act on it instantly. All you are engaging in is gathering helpful information, like a spiritual detective, by accessing the Akashic Records.

You do not need to act on the information instantly. You may have to digest it or think it over for some time. And that is okay. Do not put worthless pressure on yourself and do not scare yourself into believing that, for instance, if the Records let you know that your present job isn't in your greatest good, you will have to quit the next morning. You're still in charge of your life experience. Simply gather the information, and after that, put it to use as best you can.

Sample questions to ask the Akashic Records

Notice that many of these questions are centered on the self (they do not pry into various other people's lives, that is an enormous no!), and they're not "yes" or "no" questions.

Attempt to craft questions that will yield complex, interesting answers. While doing so, you do not wish to be too broad with questions like, "What is my soul purpose?". Sure, it sounds like a fantastic question, but something a little more precise - like, "What is my soul purpose right now?", or perhaps "What is my soul purpose as well as can I apply it?" – these questions can easily enable you to get much more clear and more helpful information.

Let us dive into the questions:

- What's my soul purpose right now?
- Just how can I better align with my soul purpose?
- How can I align my soul purpose with my job or career?
- Why have I not had the chance to recuperate problem Y or X?
- What is restricting me from manifesting higher abundance?
- What beliefs and ideas did I get from my family?
- What concepts and beliefs have I internalized from my culture?
- What function(s) did I play in my previous lives?
- Did I have a past life vow? In that case, what sort of vow? Just how can I release it in case it is not serving me?
- What's my present relationship teaching me? Am I bringing this lesson from a past life?
- What's my foremost role in this lifetime?
- Just how can I use my talents to serve others?
- Where does my addiction or behavior originate from?
- What's my addiction, compulsion, or behavior protecting me from?
- How can I release my addiction, behavior, or compulsion?
- How can I release this pattern of toxic relationships?
- Just how can I release my thoughts of shame, jealousy, anger, guilt, fear? Have I experienced those feelings in past lifetimes? Why?

- Did I understand person X in a previous lifetime? What was our connection then?
- Did I create a past life contract with person X? What was the nature of the contract?
- Just how can I release this outdated or perhaps unhelpful past-life contract?
- How can I feel pumped up about my purpose again?
- Where does my sensitivity come from? Just how can I make use of it in this lifetime?
- How can I set and enforce stronger boundaries in my life?
- Why has it been so strenuous for me to speak up and stand up for myself in this lifetime?
- Was I ever persecuted, banished, or perhaps tortured for my spiritual gifts in a past lifetime? Just how can I release that trauma and reclaim my spiritual gifts?
- Just how can I get along much better with people in this lifetime?
- Did I understand my family/relative in a past life? What was our relationship then? Why is it still carrying over now?

Using any of these questions in a new Akashic Records reading will help you access better and more valuable information.

Benefits of accessing your Akashic Records

In a nutshell, you will get to realize who you are at the Soul level. You will realize what special gifts and talents you're born with. You will become conscious, and understand that you're designed to express your talents in your physical life. You will also discover the reason that while you've wanted to express them, you have been facing certain blocks. With brand new awareness and the intent to express yourself completely in the future, you have an optimistic shift in energy consciousness.

Obvious obstacles to your present life

Working with a reading done won't be useful to you if there's absolutely nothing we can do about the blocks, restrictions, and negative influences present in your Akashic Records.

The crucial piece about reading through the Akashic Records is that it provides a clearing and cleansing out of bad influences and a realignment of your soul. Restrictions and blocks can show chakra imbalances, memory issues, bad astral travel, entity influences, program implants, negative thought forms, karma, etc. Discordant energies created can affect you, lifetime after lifetime.

Your key to leading a graceful, abundant, and peaceful life

Developing your Akashic Records and having your soul cleansed is the primary key to leading a graceful, peaceful, purposeful, and abundant life. Free from your restrictions and blocks, you have every chance to express yourself authentically based on your natural talents and gifts, and in alignment with your highest purpose and path.

The greatest part of this procedure is that you do not need to wake up from your chair to experience healing! Presently, there are no long therapy sessions to attend. Neither is some type of past life regression necessary! Your Akashic Records can be accessed very simply!

Expand your awareness: Reconnect to the source

Your soul decided to incarnate into this lifetime on Earth. It desires the experience of abundance and beauty in its physical lifetime. Nevertheless, to enter into full realization and experience, it had to forget who it was upon incarnation.

With an Akashic Record reading, you reactivate your memory. You increase your awareness. Vibrationally, your energy goes through a growth and a lift. You see obstacles less as troubles, and instead, you see them as discovering experiences. You reunite to the essence of who you are!

It's not as complicated as you think it to be. It's very simple as long as you're clear with your intentions and you're willing to accept any information the Records might give you. The next chapter talks about the Akashic Records of the Future. Always remember that having an open mind is a must when reading your Akashic Records.

Chapter 11

Akashic Records of the Future

> *"The more tranquil a man becomes, the greater is his success, his influence, his power for good"*
> James Allen

We've talked endlessly about past lives. Now, in this chapter, we're going to discuss more on how the Akashic Records contribute to our future.

The future to me is a really interesting space and what the Akashic Masters tell me is nothing is written in stone. So our future isn't written in stone in comparison to our past. We quite often feel that the past is done, so it should be written but not permanently set. It's changeable, the same as the future is. One of the more effective Akashic work I do for clients is to get into their previous lives and help clear, release, and heal the past pains and trauma, so they can move ahead and progress in this life.

As you might know, there is simply no time and space. All is taking place at a similar moment. It is unimaginable for our brains to understand that, and although I am in this energy all the time, my brain cannot grasp it either. But what I do know is that I can see and change the past. Additionally, when I do that, it changes the current moment and our power to create another option down the road.

Open your soul's path

When we release pain and fear, it helps us to be open to our soul path to change life direction and to be in alignment with a brand new, higher vibration. So, we don't know much about the future, the choices we will create, or what we and those around us will create together. You can project what is going to happen from this moment forward. If I stay walking on an extremely straight narrow path and do not turn or deviate at all, I will end up at that point directly in front of me. But if I turn, and I begin walking off one or perhaps two degrees, well, ten or twenty years down the road, I will be in a different place.

The other funny thing about us humans is, in case you tell someone their future, we usually change course by making different decisions simply because we love to be beings of free will. That is the reason we come to Earth. So in case you tell me anything in the future has already been decided, I will do all that I possibly can to prove you wrong and exercise my freedom of choice.

The way the future is changing in your Akashic Records

The potential future in Akashic Records is turning into a little bit of a jungle. That is not a terrible thing. It is a testament to how more empowered we are!

Akashic Records do not contain "our future." Rather, the Akashic Records contain ALL of our possible futures, based on our present circumstances.

Whenever we create a decision and take action, we ground one of our possible futures into our reality. A few other possible futures are then, of course, deactivated. We excluded them through our actions since we made a choice. While doing so, we produce an entire crop of new choices for ourselves; possibilities that weren't offered to us before.

This happens to be true. What is changed in the last five years is precisely how many possible futures exist to us at any given time!

As individuals, we now can influence large numbers of individuals via the Internet, should we decide to. We can have our very own TV show on YouTube. We can raise money for our small business projects via websites like Kickstarter. We have information available to us on almost anything we care to learn. All we want is the determination to take action, a bit of creativity, and life has become an assortment of possibilities.

But what I have observed in my readings lately is that all this possibility is leaving many of my clients overwhelmed and stuck.

We have all of this freedom of choice, but no one to tell us what we should do.

We have the possibility nowadays to live completely within our most divine self-expression. Yet, it leaves us scratching our heads.

Because behind the confusion is fear.

What if we choose the "wrong" possible future? What if we deselect a possibility that could have been the "best" one? How can we choose the "right" path?

We have created a world where freedom can be obtained from any person who chooses it more quickly than ever. But the lack of limitation, the absolute creativity available to us, leaves many people with a feeling of confusion and insecurity.

We have all this power.

We are simply not sure if we truly want it. Due to this, power comes with responsibility attached.

Today, we appear to collectively be in a single camp or perhaps another. We are either standing amid possibility, unwilling to choose one for fear of excluding others. Or we are progressing love gangbusters and experiencing manifestation like never before.

There's very much power inherent in our choices nowadays where taking action feels like taking a single leap of faith. When we create a decision, the Universe is very responsive and our world can shift and changes practically overnight.

With a single action, many possibilities fade away. Allowing many new ones to come into fruition.

All of this capability for change is scary. Unless we are ready to embrace it, get on the roller coaster and take the power of self-determination for a spin.

All can be obtained from us. We simply have to choose.

Akashic consultation vs. Psychic reading

People frequently ask whether an Akashic consultation differs from a psychic reading, and this is an example of my answer. A psychic reading can bring us information, yes. But, an Akashic consultation not only brings in information, it also changes the blueprint of who we are. The blueprint is changed whether we set that intention, and in case our purpose is in our best and highest interest.

You will notice I am not naming this diagnosis and keeping with the guidance someone else received. "My guides said that it was vital that she not call it X but come up with another title for it while she is going through this journey." These are the words the pupil facilitator used.

Shaping your identity

This resonates with the truth. Usually, the Records will guide us to never use labels or other words to help shape our identity. They're reminding us that once we take on an event or a diagnosis as part of who we are, it could be much more difficult to transform.

"See yourself to be an individual who doesn't have X," the Records suggest. "See yourself as a person who's healed," they continue.

How will this guidance impact the recipient? It is too soon to learn.

And, frankly, we are unlikely to know the whole story. It is difficult to say what experiences will change than what would've likely happened without this information and energy.

Nevertheless, if all possible futures have already been created, the individual much more strongly connected right now to one when she's happy and healthy once again. She's much less connected with the diagnosis and more strongly connected with health, and that can't help but promote better health for her.

Understanding the future

Among the most common challenges that many people experience regularly will be the fear of making a mistake, or perhaps an incorrect choice, which could then negatively impact them, the people they love, and their lives.

Many people think that if they could see into the future, then with no hesitation they would know what to do.

It is usually this idea of certainty as well as the drive to achieve it, which actually contribute to us feeling stuck or perhaps paralyzed into inaction; repeating unhelpful patterns and habits, or making seemingly safer decisions that do not bring us the type of happiness, fulfillment, and internal peace that we want.

It is normal and natural to wish to have the capability to have certainty over our future and our lives. This propensity is conditioned into us, generation after generation, without us even realizing the degree of its influence and the limitations it produces in our lives.

Regrettably, if this desire comes from fear, the process of actually accessing reliable and grounded information that is valuable about the future becomes compromised and undermines the quality of our capacity and consciousness to make discerning and wise choices.

It is uncomplicated to find out how you can access supportive, useful, and practical information that may help us develop the future we want without involving fear.

The future isn't something permanently fixed. The future is a place of potentiality that remains until we begin focusing on one of these capacities with intention and determination, and we start shaping it.

Quantum Physics has been in a position to confirm that the outcomes of any experiment are generally susceptible to its observer(s) and that the aim of the observer(s) can change the outcomes of that experiment, as demonstrated in the double-slit experiment.

Practically speaking, this implies that you, as the observer of your life, have influence and power over the outcomes in your life. What you think and feel regularly influences what happens next, i.e., your future.

This means that you can negatively or positively impact your future if you begin thinking and feeling differently from what you have.

Whenever we spend time worrying about something, feeling unsure, or perhaps projecting negative potentials into the future, is time that we do not get to spend feeling great about ourselves or our lives, and we are unable to prioritize what's significant to us; letting go of the past, feeling and being inventive, and empowering ourselves towards our goals and intentions.

In this fearful state, we create numerous mysteries about the future. We have limited access to what would typically be offered to us in the form of beneficial and accurate information about the future.

What sort of future do you believe will be created through the lens of our self-doubt and fear?

Almost certainly, one with similar fearful and doubtful limitations that were initially produced within our very mind.

In our personal experience, the most effective way to get to know and understand the future is by creating it in the current moment.

The current moment is exactly where all of your power of influence is. The same as how the present moment we experience is a consequence of the past and the future is made in the present moment.

You have influence and power in creating your future, therefore, the more energy you put towards building the future in the current moment, the more influence you are going to have over the process and the effects you get.

It is possible to boost this procedure and amplify your power of influence over your life and your future.

One way of accomplishing this target is by accessing and receiving information from your spirit guides and other informed beings. Having the ability to hear this information is tuning a lot of love into a certain radio channel.

It is feasible to quiet our minds, to silence our fears, and also to become optimally grounded and open in our hearts so that we are in a position to receive guidance and wisdom which may help us make wiser, conscious, more discerning, and loving decisions in our lives.

One particular method of getting there is from the Akashic Records, which could be viewed as a register of everything that has ever happened and will happen in the Universe.

This information can be obtained if there is one thing that is meaningful to you and if you see the importance of receiving such guidance in your decision-making process and creating your future.

When we gain an unbiased and comprehensive understanding of the implications of the options that we make on ourselves and others as well as our lives, it becomes far simpler to make choices that we feel at ease with as well as to have confidence in our process of decision making.

Are there questions the Akashic Records can't answer?

When we first become associated with the Akashic Records and learn this amazing storehouse of information about the planet and ourselves, it can feel both empowering and consuming as we're tempted to find out about everyone and everything at once. But can the Records answer every one of our questions?

In principle, yes. But in practice, this will depend on our vibrational alignment.

While it's a fact that the Akashic Records are a high vibrational library that is present outside the boundaries of space and time, we the people who access them, continue to have time and space to cope with. To know how the reading works and what information type we can access, we first have to discover what the Akashic Records are.

I believe it's helpful to think of the Records as a library without taking the metaphor too literally.

Like any library, the Records require a method to use the information to get appropriate and useful answers. The same as any library, the Records contain knowledge that we do not need.

If I needed to flip through a book on astrophysics or quantum mechanics, so long as I'm in a position to read, I will certainly discover new information and be able to put it into practice, then I will not go far. I'd need to have studied these subjects to learn the information in the books. In the Akashic Records, we only get the information that we can process and understand at our present development level.

As someone who carries out healing and readings in the Records, I do get questions that I can't answer. Sometimes the reason is exposed to me; at times, it's not.

In many circumstances, these can be ineffective questions that may connect to future events, which are being established in the now. Learning about the future may prevent the hunter from taking the most spiritually productive course of action, or disrupt a lesson the soul has contracted to find out. Occasionally, it's much more reliable to do recovery work, which would move the viewpoint.

There's a reason predicting the future is discouraged in many religious traditions. While there are effective ways of future predictions, like prophetic revelations or visions, we have to keep in mind that the goal of these predictions happens to be present a chance in altering the present course of action and warn us to stay away from a bad future outcome. Put simply, predictions were made to ensure that the future can be modified. This is very distinct from predictions that take our power away.

Nobody and nothing can give your power of co-creation away! We produce our future by the choices we make in the now. We often do it as a cumulative, as we do not exist in a vacuum, the duty is typically far more distinct, but nothing is set in stone.

Naturally, some future trajectories are obvious. In case you mess with the common laws, you are going to be in trouble. Or if you neglect an action, you won't achieve anything. Sometimes a situation isn't what it appears to us, and we're guided to find out that what another person or what we are doing is unfruitful and won't result in the desired outcome. If we're entirely detached from the outcome and are lined up with our soul, we will likely get detailed guidance about the future.

What better serves us is cultivating trust in comparison to dependence on predictions.

I've come across many unproductive concerns in reading. These consist of, "When will I fulfill my soulmate, twin flame, husband, etc.? Do I have a twin flame someplace out there?

When will we connect again? Do you think I need to pursue this specific relationship? What are my possibilities with this man or woman?"

While I don't discount the validity of these questions and have asked them myself when I was eager for guidance, the matter isn't the questions themselves. The matter is the underlying motive of the seeker.

An Akashic Record reading isn't a psychic reading. It's first and foremost a spiritual activation. Your soul growth isn't served by knowing if you have a twin flame. It's, served by realizing you're lonely and seek fulfillment outside of yourself (and the Divine). Providing you let that happen, you won't ever visit your twin flame, whether you have them or not.

Naturally, some situations require a lot more nuanced guidance, and lots of seemingly unproductive questions have validity in context. As one of my friends says, "The one dumb question will be the one you did not ask."

You will find no dumb questions in the Records, but what we have to understand is that we're approaching a higher dimensional space where everything is seen from another perspective. Several of our concerns are turned around, and we're guided to new levels of understanding and being. Indeed, at times, rather than responses, we get many more questions on the spiritual path. But the Akashic Records don't dispense the information indiscriminately. We have to grow into them, not them into us.

There are many possibilities in our life, and it's our choice which one to take. The Akashic Records serve as a guide to our decisions, but it's still our choice if we choose to act upon the information that we get.

Conclusion

The Akashic Records aren't a place beyond the reach of mere mortals but are accessible to everyone. It's usual for individuals to go there frequently during sleep to process experiences that they've had and receive more support and training. But when interpreted through dreams, they frequently disappear from conscious memory once the waking mind goes back to the fore. To reach the Akashic Records with the conscious mind takes practice and training, but doors open to wisdom and healing that people never thought they might achieve. Whether you work with somebody who could access the Akashic Records for you, or you find out the way to reach them yourself, reconnecting with your real self and experiencing who you genuinely are will change your life.

Sharon Copeland

Lightning Source UK Ltd.
Milton Keynes UK
UKHW022045270921
391272UK00010B/2318